Canadian Biography Series

NORTHROP FRYE: A VISIONARY LIFE

Frye in the mid-seventies

Northrop Frye

A VISIONARY LIFE

Joseph Adamson

ECW PRESS

Copyright © ECW PRESS, 1993

CANADIAN CATALOGUING IN PUBLICATION DATA

Adamson, Joseph, 1950–
Northrop Frye : a visionary life

(Canadian biography series)
ISBN 1-55022-184-1

1. Frye, Northrop, 1912–1991. 2. Critics – Canada – Biography.
3. College teachers – Canada – Biography. I. Title. II. Series:
Canadian biography series (Toronto, Ont.).

PN75.F7A4 1993   801'.95'092   C93-094544-1

This book has been published with the assistance of the
Ministry of Culture and Communications of the Province
of Ontario, through funds provided by the Ontario
Publishing Centre, and with the assistance of grants from
the Department of Communications, The Canada Council, the
Ontario Arts Council, and the Government of Canada through
the Canadian Studies and Special Projects Directorate of the
Department of the Secretary of State of Canada.

Design and imaging by ECW Type & Art, Oakville, Ontario.
Printed by Imprimerie Gagné, Louiseville, Québec.

Distributed by General Publishing Co. Limited,
30 Lesmill Road, Toronto, Ontario M3B 2T6,
(416) 445-3333, (800) 387-0172 (Canada), FAX (416) 445-5967.

Distributed to the trade in the United States exclusively by
InBook, 140 Commerce Street, P.O. Box 120261,
East Haven, Connecticut, U.S.A. 06512,
(203) 467-4257, FAX (203) 469-7697
Customer service: 1-800-253-3605 or 1-800-243-0138.

Published by ECW PRESS,
1980 Queen Street East, Toronto, Ontario Canada M4L 1J2

ACKNOWLEDGEMENTS

I would like to thank the Victoria University Library (Toronto) for permission to consult and to quote from its collection of materials pertaining to Northrop Frye. Unless otherwise indicated, all cited letters are from the library's collection. I would also like to thank the library for permission to use the photographs reproduced here. I owe a great debt to the helpful service provided by the library staff, and I would like to express my gratitude in particular to Irene Dutton and Dolores Signori for their kind assistance.

I would like to thank the executors of Northrop Frye's estate for permission to quote from his letters to Helen Kemp Frye, and the Pierpont-Morgan Library for permission to use the reproduction of the engraving from Blake's illustrations of *The Book of Job*.

Although I have not referred specifically to the scholarship of Robert Denham, his groundbreaking study, *Northrop Frye and Critical Method*, has helped to shape and sharpen my general understanding of Frye's work. I have also made use of his *Northrop Frye: An Annotated Bibliography*, which has been an indispensable research tool and a great aid in matters of documentation.

For many of the factual details I have relied on John Ayre's landmark work, *Northrop Frye: A Biography*, and I would like to acknowledge here my indebtedness to his exhaustive research, without which my own book would not have been possible.

I would like to thank Jane Widdicombe for her help with some factual details.

Finally, I am grateful to Jeffery Donaldson and Jean Wilson for reading the manuscript so carefully and with such discrimination; their many suggestions have been invaluable.

PHOTOGRAPHS: Cover photo, 1977, Chris McDonald, is used by permission of Victoria University Library (Northrop Frye Collection); frontispiece illustration 1975[?], Lutz Dille, is used by permission of Victoria University Library (Northrop Frye Collection); illustration 2, 1919, photographer unknown, is used by permission of Victoria University Library (Northrop Frye Collection); illustration 3, 1933, George Freeland, is used by permission of Victoria University Library (Northrop Frye Collection); illustration 4, 1937, photographer unknown, is used by permission of Victoria University Library (Northrop Frye Collection); illustration 5,

1947, John Steele, is used by permission of Victoria University Library (Northrop Frye Collection); illustration 6, 1959, photographer unknown, is used by permission of Victoria University Library (Northrop Frye Collection); illustration 7 is used by permission of the Pierpont-Morgan Library; illustration 8, date unknown, photographer unknown, is used by permission of Victoria University Library (Northrop Frye Collection); illustration 9, 1983, Steve Behal, is used by permission of Victoria University Library (Northrop Frye Collection); illustration 10, 1983, Robert Lansdale, is used by permission of Victoria University Library (Northrop Frye Collection); illustration 11, 1967, F. Roy Kemp, is used by permission of Victoria University Library (Northrop Frye Collection); illustration 12, 1974, photographer unknown, is used by permission of Victoria University Library (Northrop Frye Collection); illustration 13, 1981, Robert Lansdale, is used by permission of Victoria University Library (Northrop Frye Collection); illustration 14, 1988, photographer unknown, is used by permission of Victoria University Library (Northrop Frye Collection); illustration 15, 1988, photographer unknown, is used by permission of Victoria University Library (Northrop Frye Collection).

TABLE OF CONTENTS

LIST OF ILLUSTRATIONS

A person's real self is perhaps more clearly evoked by what other people think of him than by his own analysis of himself. The "real me" may be a layer of personae, the relationships with other people.

The "real me" may be the work, then, and not the person at all.

Yes, I think that is true. Somebody was in my office the other day urging me to write my autobiography. What I couldn't explain to him is that everything I write *I* consider autobiography, although nobody else would.

—Northrop Frye (*On Education* 211)

Chronology

1912   Born on 14 July, in Sherbrooke, Quebec. Son of Herman Edward Frye and Catherine Maud Howard, the youngest of three children (his sister Vera, the middle child, is 12 years old at the time). Both parents are devoutly Methodist.

1917   His brother, Howard, is killed in action in the First World War.

1919   With the failure of his father's business, the family moves to Moncton, New Brunswick, where Herman Frye becomes a hardware salesman for the Maritimes.

1928   Graduates from Aberdeen High School, and in the fall takes a three-month secretarial training course at Success Business College.

1929   In September, enters Victoria College, University of Toronto. In October, the stock market crashes.

1930   In the summer, working at the Central Reference Library, discovers Denis Saurat's *Blake and Modern Thought* and starts reading Blake. In the fall of his second year at Vic, meets Helen Kemp. Takes Pelham Edgar's Shakespeare course. Discovers Oswald Spengler's *The Decline of the West* in the Hart House Library.

1933   Graduates with an honours degree in Philosophy and English. In the fall, enters Emmanuel College, University of Toronto, as a theological student to prepare for ministry in the United Church of Canada.

1934   In addition to his studies at Emmanuel, presents a seminar on Blake's *Milton* in Herbert Davis's graduate class, with Pelham Edgar in attendance. Spends five months (May to September) as a student minister on a mission field in rural Saskatchewan. The experience convinces Frye that he is not suited for the ministry.

1934–35 Helen Kemp spends a year at the Courtauld Institute in London. In the fall of 1934, Frye reads Sir James Frazer's *The Golden Bough* and Émile Mâle's *The Gothic Image.*

1935–36 Spends his first full year of teaching at the University of Toronto. In the spring, ordained as a minister in the United Church of Canada. First essays published in the *Canadian Forum.*

1936–37 Travels to England to study for a degree in English literature at Merton College, Oxford University. His tutor is Edmund Blunden. Attends lectures by C.S. Lewis.

1937 Spends part of the summer touring Italy with friends from Oxford. Returns to Toronto, and marries Helen Kemp on 24 August.

1937–38 Takes up a one-year appointment as "special lecturer" at Victoria College.

1938 Returns to Oxford to complete his degree. Makes a month-long tour of Paris and environs with friends over the Christmas holiday.

1939 On 20 June, appointed a member of the permanent staff at Victoria College. In the summer, tours Italy with Helen and friends. Returns to England and leaves for Canada on 12 August, less than three weeks before the outbreak of war.

1942 Promoted to assistant professor. Publishes "Music in Poetry" and "Anatomy in Prose Fiction," his first major articles, in the *University of Toronto Quarterly* and the *Manitoba Arts Review.*

1946 Promoted to associate professor.

1947 Publishes *Fearful Symmetry*, a study of William Blake. Promoted to full professor.

1948 Becomes managing editor of the *Canadian Forum*, a position he will hold until 1952. In September,

	presents "The Argument of Comedy" at the English Institute.
1950	Granted a Guggenheim fellowship to write a study of Spenser.
1951	Publishes "The Archetypes of Literature," the so-called mini-anatomy, in *Kenyon Review*. "Letters in Canada: 1950, Poetry," appears, the first of 10 annual surveys of Canadian poetry that Frye will write over the next decade for the *University of Toronto Quarterly*. Elected Fellow of the Royal Society of Canada.
1952	Becomes chair of the Department of English at Victoria College.
1953	Serves as chair of the English Institute.
1954	Appointed Class of 1932 Visiting Lecturer at Princeton University. *Anatomy of Criticism* is an expansion of the four public lectures delivered there in March.
1957	Publishes *Anatomy of Criticism*, a landmark study of structural poetics. Appointed visiting lecturer at Harvard University.
1959	Becomes principal of Victoria College, serving until 1967.
1962	Presents "The Drunken Boat: The Revolutionary Element in Romanticism" at a conference on Romanticism he chairs at the English Institute; the other participants are M.H. Abrams, Lionel Trilling, and René Wellek. The proceedings are edited by Frye and published as *Romanticism Reconsidered* (1963).
1963	Publishes *The Well-Tempered Critic*; *The Educated Imagination*, a series of talks aired by the CBC; *Fables of Identity*, a collection of essays; and *T.S. Eliot*, which provokes letters of outrage and protest from the publisher, Faber and Faber, and from Eliot himself.
1965	In September, the English Institute holds a special session devoted to Frye, with a panel composed of Angus Fletcher, Murray Krieger, Geoffrey Hartman,

and W.K. Wimsatt. Frye publishes *A Natural Perspective*, a study of Shakespeare's comedies, and *The Return of Eden*, a study of Milton.

1967   Appointed University Professor at the University of Toronto (the first person to receive such an appointment). Establishes an office at Massey College. Jane (Welch) Widdicombe, who becomes his secretary, will remain his invaluable assistant until his death. Publishes *Fools of Time*, a study of Shakespeare's tragedies, and *The Modern Century*.

1968   Publishes *A Study of English Romanticism*. Appointed member of the Canadian Radio-Television and Telecommunications Commission, serving until 1977.

1969   Begins to work on a successor to *Anatomy*, a study of the myth of concern that grows into the two books on the Bible.

1970   Publishes *The Stubborn Structure*, a collection of essays.

1971   Publishes *The Bush Garden*, a collection of reviews and essays on Candian literature, and *The Critical Path*, an extended essay on the myth of concern.

1972   Made a Companion of the Order of Canada.

1975   Appointed Charles Eliot Norton Professor of Poetry, Harvard University.

1976   Elected president of the Modern Language Association. Publishes *The Secular Scripture*, a study of romance, and *Spiritus Mundi*, a collection of essays on literature, myth, and society.

1978   Named chancellor of Victoria University.

1979   Gives an extensive lecture tour of Italy, speaking in Milan, Florence, Padua, Vicenza, Venice, Urbino, and Rome.

1980   Publishes *Creation and Recreation*.

1982   Publishes *The Great Code*, his first study of the Bible.

1983   Publishes *The Myth of Deliverance*, a study of Shakespeare's "problem" comedies. *Centre and*

	Labyrinth, a Festschrift in Frye's honour, is published by friends and colleagues at Victoria College.
1986	Death of Helen Frye in Australia during Frye's tour of Australian universities.
1987	Wins the Governor General's Award for Non-Fiction for *Northrop Frye on Shakespeare,* a collection of essays based on his undergraduate lectures on Shakespeare's plays. In May, attends an international conference on his work in Rome.
1988	Marries Elizabeth Brown on 27 July.
1990	Publishes *Words with Power,* his second study of the Bible.
1991	Dies, 23 January. A family funeral is held in the Victoria College Chapel on 26 January; a memorial service for the Victoria University community is held in the same location on 28 January. The following day, a memorial service for the larger community is held in Convocation Hall at the University of Toronto, with the Lieutenant Governor of Ontario in attendance, and many testimonial speakers, including Bob Rae (Premier of Ontario), Margaret Atwood, Pauline McGibbon, and Pierre Juneau. Blake's "Jerusalem" is sung by the congregation at the end of the service. *The Double Vision* appears posthumously, only months after his death.

Northrop Frye

A VISIONARY LIFE

Beginnings

Herman Northrop Frye was born in Sherbrooke, Quebec, 14 July 1912, to Catherine ("Cassie") Maud Howard and Herman Edward Frye. His father's family were farmers from Massachusetts, thought to be descendants of the Puritan "ffrie" who had come over as a dissenter from England in the 1630 migration. Herman Frye was in the hardware business, where his lack of success left the family in a "state of shabby genteel poverty" (*In Conversation* 43). They were forced to change residence frequently; when Herman's business failed, they moved to nearby Lennoxville. When Frye was seven, they settled in Moncton, where his father worked as a hardware salesman for the Maritimes.

Catherine Frye was the daughter of a Methodist preacher who moved from parish to parish in eastern Ontario and the Eastern Townships of Quebec. The religious background on both sides of Frye's family encouraged a mental attitude that he was later to define, in opposition to T.S. Eliot's "Classical, royalist, and Anglo-Catholic" biases, as "Protestant, radical, and Romantic" (*Fables* 149). In particular, his mother's inculcation of Methodist views, in combination with her liberal encouragement of artistic pursuits, undoubtedly did much to sow the seeds of the apocalyptic social vision that is so apparent in Frye's understanding of literature. "In Methodism," he wrote at the other end of his life, even of the episcopal variety to which my family belonged, there was an emphasis on religious experience as distinct from doctrine and on very early exposure to the story element in the Bible. Such a conditioning may have helped to propel me in the direction of a literary criticism that has kept revolving around the Bible, not as a source of doctrine but as a source of story and vision. (*Double* 3)

Catherine was 41 when Northrop, the third and last child in the family, was born. His sister, Vera, was 12 years older. The eldest child, Howard, was killed in 1917 in the First World War at the age of 19, and Catherine was grief-stricken. When the family moved to Moncton, two years later, she was separated from old friends and felt exiled. With the subsequent loss of her hearing, she became "withdrawn and introverted"; Frye's father, on the other hand, had always been "of a rather retiring disposition socially" (*In Conversation* 42). Frye's consequent isolation as a child, reinforced by his family's poverty and by his own extremely bookish temperament and physical awkwardness, may have been the most important psychological factor in his upbringing: "I suppose I spent the first seventeen years of my life mooning. When there is no world to live in except the world of the imagination, naturally that's going to take shape" (43).

"Mooning," as Frye calls it, meant an introverted reliance on literature and music. Frye learned to read very early; at the age of four (legend has it), his favourite book was *Pilgrim's Progress*.[1] He showed musical talent as well, and became a very good pianist. In high school, his music teacher, George Ross, a student of Sir Hubert Parry, "had a tremendous influence" on him, "not so much from what he said or did but simply from the authority which he carried from knowing his subject" ("Music" 270). Ross taught in such a way that "the only authority that came through was the authority of music itself" ("Moncton" 331). Exemplifying for Frye the ability to become "a transparent instrument" of one's subject (335), he presented him with an enduring pedagogical ideal. For Frye, interestingly enough, music, and not literature, was "the great area of emotional and imaginative discovery" (331). His love and

18

FIGURE 2

Frye in Moncton, 34 North Street, circa 1919.

appreciation of music would stay with him throughout his life; throughout his career, his acute sense of musical structure supplied him with an important analogy for the structural patterns of literature.[2]

From an early age Frye seems also to have been sensitive to the visual arts. His later interest in Blake's engravings, medieval religious art, and surrealist painting (an interest encouraged by his wife, Helen Kemp, who was an art student before their marriage) is one more indication of Frye's interdisciplinary scope, which has its deepest roots in the world of culture to which he was exposed as a child.[3]

The one physical activity that Frye greatly enjoyed was bicycling, and he spent endless hours riding and exploring the countryside around Moncton. This simple pastime sparked his imagination as well: "I think that I always tended to create a kind of fairytale world around me, and every road, every dirt road going into the country seemed to me to be wrapped in mystery" ("Moncton" 336).

Frye had an important experience as an adolescent, analogous to a conversion in its intensity, which led him to reject the mindless literalism that he often encountered at church and school. He recalls walking to high school one day, and suddenly feeling as if

> that whole shitty and smelly garment (of fundamentalist teaching I had all my life) just dropped off into the sewers and stayed there. It was like the Bunyan feeling, about the burden of sin falling off his back only with me it was a burden of anxiety. Anything might have touched it off, but I don't know what specifically did, or if anything did. I just remember that suddenly that was no longer a part of me and would never be again. (qtd. in Ayre 44)

Given his later view that pulling away from all social anxiety is the kernel of imaginative vision in culture, it is hardly surprising that Frye found his schooling before university a largely painful experience. He later wrote of a "penal quality which universal compulsory education necessarily has attached to it," a quality associated with "certain visions of my own childhood days. . . . I saw children lined up and marched into a grimy brick building," after which "the educational process began" (*Divisions* 139–40). Needless to say, an "atmosphere of the classroom [that] came to resemble that of an armed truce" (140) could hardly have done much to awaken Frye's mind and imagination. In these early years, encouraged by his mother (who had been a teacher before she married), Frye became responsible for his own education, largely through wide and eclectic reading. As a high-school student, his favourite author was George Bernard Shaw. The affinity is understandable: Frye would share with the playwright a distinct fondness for the conventions of romantic comedy, as well as a finely honed wit.

On graduation from Aberdeen High School in Moncton, Frye won a scholarship to a local business college, where he became an excellent typist. In the spring of 1929, he entered a typing contest in Toronto, and did well enough to be a finalist. He then planned to go to Victoria College, and was accepted into the Pass Course on probation (high school in New Brunswick was two years short of the requirements in Ontario). By a happy coincidence, another typing contest was to take place in Toronto in September, and the business college agreed to cover the significant expense of his train fare. On 18 September, at the age of 17, he left Moncton to begin his university education.

Victoria was the United Church college at the University of Toronto (and the Methodist college before church union in 1925); it was the obvious place for a young Canadian intellectual and potential ministerial candidate of Frye's particular background to take his undergraduate education. His experience there was decisive. Isolated and socially inactive as a boy in Moncton, he now "flung [himself] into every kind of student activity" ("Moncton" 336). In the next few years, along with a growing sense of belonging came the basic intellectual insights that were to stay with him throughout his life. Frye would always insist on the continuity and relative permanence of literary conventions, and this fundamental aspect of his critical thinking seems to have been reflected in his life as well; he was to feel so rooted at Victoria College and its environs that he would never leave, despite many tempting offers to do so.

No one, Frye wrote in 1968, "who knew the teachers I had at

21

Victoria . . . would be in the least surprised at any student's wanting to pursue the careers they were so brilliant an advertisement for" (*Bush* 182). The reference is primarily to the "extraordinary trio" formed by E.J. Pratt, Pelham Edgar, and J.D. Robins. Pratt had been an instructor in psychology whom Edgar discovered and persuaded to change vocation. Frye's developing critical views found confirmation in the imaginative vision that would win the poet a preeminent place in the history of Canadian literature. Robins was an Old English scholar and an empathic and popular teacher, whose unorthodox interest in folk literature stimulated Frye's appreciation of primitive forms of literary expression. Edgar — to whom *Fearful Symmetry* is dedicated — seems to have had the greatest influence on Frye. At the time, Victoria College had the reputation of being a place where teaching was especially valued and where the student's personal dialogue with literature was encouraged. One of Frye's classmates, Pauline McGibbon (later to become Lieutenant Governor of Ontario), remembers: "The story was that Norrie had read everything in Shakespeare before he ever came to the university, and so he was the only one who could really talk back and forth and question Pelham Edgar, while the rest of us sat there like nincompoops and just listened to the two of them" (qtd. in Cayley 9). The lesson of his teachers was not lost. Doubtless, Frye's later attempts in the classroom to engage his own students in dialogue were often frustrated by his intimidating reputation, which his shyness did little to dispel. But the effort to communicate was always intense, even in the notorious awkwardness of the "long pauses" in his lectures. According to Frye, this came partly out of respect for the students: "I'm listening to the echo of [the author's work] from my students. It takes a long time for that to penetrate, to percolate through my students" (*In Conversation* 148). As his mentors did before him, he would insist that students encounter the work on their own terms, without any interference from secondary sources, an unnecessary distraction that Frye himself learned to dispense with at an early stage in his career.

When Frye completed his BA in 1933, graduating first in the honours course in Philosophy and English, he found himself at a crossroads. Lacking the financial resources to pursue his

FIGURE 3

Frye's graduation photo. Victoria College, 1933.

studies, he spent the summer in Moncton, unsure of how he would be able to continue at the university. Friends at Victoria College managed to find the funds, and he was able to return to Toronto to complete a degree in theology at Emmanuel College. The chief function of Emmanuel, the theological school affiliated with Victoria, was to prepare students for ministry in the United Church of Canada. However, Frye's growing interest in the study of literature now drew him irresistibly in another direction. His miserable experience as a student minister in the summer of 1934, when for five months he served in a remote part of the Saskatchewan prairies, made it painfully clear to him how unsuited he was to the ministry. Indeed, by the time he decided to be ordained, in 1936, some felt that he should be excluded in light of his undisguised intention not to become an active clergyman.

The most important factor, however, in Frye's complete conversion to academic life was William Blake. Years earlier, in the summer of 1930 — while working at the Central Reference Library — Frye had discovered Denis Saurat's *Blake and Modern Thought*, and he had begun to read the relatively obscure English poet with great fervour, haunted by the feeling that he had found a visionary whose work was a riddle that he desperately needed to unlock. Blake was the angel he was to wrestle with and would not release until he was blessed. "I date everything," he said in an interview at the end of his life, "from my discovery of Blake as an undergraduate and graduate student. Everything of Blake that I could understand convinced me that his mysterious poems would be worth working at" (*On Education* 211).

In addition to his studies at Emmanuel, Frye participated in a graduate class held by Herbert Davis, a Swift scholar, who was another important mentor. It was in this course on Blake, in 1934, with Pelham Edgar in attendance, that Frye gave what must have been a most remarkable seminar. From all accounts, it was a presentation of the central vision that was later to be fully articulated in *Fearful Symmetry*, and thus arguably the kernel of his entire life's work. Frye describes the experience of writing the paper (which was on Blake's *Milton*), sitting down to work

as was my regular bad habit in those days, the night before.
. . . Around about three in the morning a different kind of
intuition hit me, though it would take me twenty years to
articulate it. The two poets [Milton and Blake] were connected by the *same* thing, and sameness leads to individual
variety, just as likeness leads to monotony. I began dimly
to see that the principle pulling me away from the historical period was the principle of mythological framework.
The Bible had provided a frame of mythology for European
poets: an immense number of critical problems began to
solve themselves as soon as one realized this. (*Spiritus* 17)

Frye has described this insight elsewhere as a moment in which
"suddenly the universe just broke open, and I've never been, as
they say, the same since" (*In Conversation* 47). It was an
explosive "feeling of an enormous number of things making
sense that had been scattered and unrelated before, a vision of
coherence" (47). Frye's work seems to have unfolded from such
epiphanies as from a series of centres: "I've had two or three
nights where I have had sudden visions of that kind. They were
I suppose ultimately visions of what I myself might be able to
do" (47). Thirteen years later, he published the book on Blake
that had been conceived at that moment; 10 years after that, he
published *Anatomy of Criticism*, which detailed the complex
relationship between Western literature and the mythological
framework that took hold in his mind that night; and at the end
of his career, he produced two books on the Bible, which was
the ultimate source of the coherence and unity that he had
glimpsed 40 years before.

Rage for Order

One thing that Blake taught Frye was that the imagined reality
that art and literature put before our eyes is of intense human
concern and, ultimately, the vision of a social ideal. Frye came
of age as an intellectual during the Depression, in the midst of

a social climate that he describes at the end of his life with
ironic hindsight:

When I arrived at Victoria College as a freshman in September 1929, North America was not only prosperous but in a
nearly hysterical state of self-congratulation. It was widely
predicted that the end of poverty and the levelling out of
social inequalities were practically within reach. In the
Soviet Union, on the other hand, the reports were mainly
of misery and despair. The inference for general public
opinion on this side of the Atlantic was clear: capitalism
worked and Marxism didn't. (Double 3–4)

Then "came the stock market crash, and there was no more
talk of capitalist Utopia" (4). At the end of that decade, in the
summer of 1939, having completed his degree at Oxford and
having just been appointed lecturer at Victoria College, Frye
cut short his tour of the cultural treasures of Italy, returning
home with war about to break out in Europe. His years of
education, in other words, were framed by two of the greatest
catastrophes in the "dissolving phantasmagoria" of a generally
"ghastly century" (In Conversation 149).

Frye's political sympathies during the thirties were clearly
socialist. The mid-thirties was a period when, "at least in the
student circles [he] was attached to . . . it was a generally
accepted dogma that capitalism had had its day and was certain
to evolve very soon, with or without a revolution, into socialism, socialism being assumed to be both a more efficient and a
morally superior system" (Double 4). He had friends who were
communists or communist sympathizers, which at that time
meant allegiance to Stalinism. However, he viewed Marxism
as an ideology that ultimately only made sense within the
larger Judeo-Christian framework of Western culture derived
from the Bible. His point, confessedly anti-historical, is that the
Marxist vision of an eventual end to history and a withering
away of all oppressive social structures has analogues in both
the Christian apocalypse and the Messianic vision of Jewish
prophecy, which together form the mythological context of
historical understanding in the West. It is the "comic" shape

that Marxism, like Christianity, attempts to give to history that intrigued Frye, who himself remained throughout his life committed to a view of literature that was prophetic and social in scope.

This social commitment was reflected in Frye's long-standing involvement in the *Canadian Forum*, which in the thirties and beyond was "a leading intellectual organ of the Canadian left" (Balfour 67), its roots planted in the social movement of the CCF. Frye was a frequent contributor to the magazine for many years, and served as its managing editor from 1948 to 1952. His leftist sympathies, however, did not prevent him from resisting the solicitations of Communist Party members because of what he saw as the party's woeful lack of imaginative vision. When Helen Kemp wrote him to from London in 1935, where she was studying at the Courtauld Institute, and expressed a growing sympathy with the communist view, he passionately wrote back:

> Obviously the world is entering a prodigious change, but the new morality will have to do something better than a rehash of the vague deistic and utilitarian sentimentalism of the very capitalistic system the Communists are most concerned to attack. There will have to be something better, for me, than the communistic exploiting of emotion by intellect. Read Blake or go to Hell: that's my message to the modern world.[4]

The wheel of history would make a complete turn in Frye's own lifetime, over half a century later, as a new period of self-congratulation, analogous to the reckless optimism of the twenties, loomed on the horizon at the end of the eighties: "That cycle has completed itself, and once again people in the West are saying, as they said sixty years ago, that it has been proved that capitalism works and that Marxism does not" (*Double* 4). Frye can thus speak with some authority, in a cautious and at times even despairing tone, of the ironies of history or, as he puts it, the "whirligig of time," and of the limited effectiveness of ideology in overcoming social oppression. Ideology, as he was able to witness at first hand, is inevitably a debasement of the authentic imaginative form that myth takes in literature, myths being "the functional units of human society, even when they are absurd myths" (*Double* 4). The real enemy in the thirties and forties was fascism, a danger that Frye was alert to as early as 1934. As a student minister in Saskatchewan, he preached a sermon in which he spoke of "a new kind of idolatry": with the collapse of superstition appears "the worship of men instead of God. The present trend to dictatorships is therefore idolatry, and there is nothing to save us from the same progression toward the evil, which is why Hitler and Co. appeal to the worst and cruellest instincts of mankind."[5] During the war, Frye passionately insisted on the pivotal role of art and literature in combating not only the immediate fascist threat, but also any authoritarian world state or order that might emerge, whatever its political or ideological stripe. In 1940, in the *Canadian Forum*, he underlined the danger of all "efforts of an organized social will to compel human life and science to fit a certain pattern of ideas" ("War" 283) and declared, "In the present war it is our business to disintegrate and disorganize this world state *whatever else happens*" (286). As a young critic and intellectual, Frye defined himself in passionate opposition to the conservative, reactionary, and even fascist tendencies of so many of the main literary figures of the thirties, such as Pound, Wyndham Lewis, Yeats, and Eliot. Frye was appalled by the sympathy for Nazism that he found in England. His tutor at Oxford, where he took a degree in English literature after graduating from Emmanuel College, was Edmund Blunden. Blunden's rather thoughtless and shortsighted admiration for Hitler, however negligible in the depth of its conviction, reflected a surprisingly prevalent envy in pre-war Britain of Nazi economic and political successes. The implications of the events that were to tear Europe apart weighed on Frye during his two years at Oxford, and his extensive travelling with friends on the continent, especially in Italy, gave him a clear glimpse of the dark portentousness of the growing crisis.

It is significant that T.S. Eliot was the only twentieth-century author to whom Frye devoted a book-length study. The book, published in 1963, offers, among other things, a systematic debunking of Eliot's often repugnant critical and social views. Not surprisingly, Eliot and his publisher, Faber and Faber, reacted with letters of protest and outrage.[6] Frye's quarrel with Eliot had to do with their extremely divergent views of the function of art and culture. With the publication of *After Strange Gods* (1934) and its anti-Semitic and generally racist conception of culture, Eliot's pronouncements had become, in Frye's opinion, despicable. The book, which he read when he was quite young and felt was "a betrayal," made him dramatically aware of his "own responsibilities as a critic" (*In Conversation* 107).[7]

The differences Frye had with Eliot, however, touched only the latter's literary and cultural criticism. Indeed, the book is a concise but comprehensive study of the coherent structure of imagery in Eliot's poetry. It is clear proof that Frye practised what he preached when he spoke of avoiding the evaluative fallacy in literary criticism. Nor should Frye's sharp divisions with Eliot divert us from recognizing the profound convergence of their concerns. The historical context in which Frye emerged as a thinker was one in which Eliot was perhaps the preeminent literary figure. Frye's early interest in myth was entirely consonant with the archetypal imagery in *The Waste Land*, much of it "stolen," in Eliot's positive sense of transformative appropriation, from scholarly works, such as Jessie Weston's *From Ritual to Romance* and Sir James Frazer's *The Golden Bough*. Furthermore when, in "Tradition and the Individual Talent," Eliot argues that the originality of a new work of art depends on a larger cultural development that "abandons nothing *en route*, which does not superannuate either Shakespeare, or Homer, or the rock drawing of the Magdalenian draughtsman" (39), he anticipates Frye's own conviction that communication in literature is based on convention, and that any new utterance must take place within the existing "order of words," as he would call it in the *Anatomy*. Whatever development there is, this development, in Eliot's words, "is not, from the point of view of the artist, any improvement" ("Tradition" 39). Frye too would insist on the stability of the arts throughout history.

The thirties were a period of intense intellectual growth for Frye, a time in which he underwent a dramatic "process of transmission by seed" (*Spiritus* 12), to use his own expression for the work of influence. It was a process activated by immense reading, and it was stimulated in particular when he began teaching. His first year of full-time teaching was in 1935–36; then, in 1937–38, before returning to Oxford to complete his degree, he replaced his friend Roy Daniells, who had left Vic to take a position at the University of Manitoba. He later reflected, "I was interested in everything, everything seemed to have some relevance to my interest, and yet the pursuit of knowledge in all directions at once was impracticable. Ever since then, I have realized that scholarship is as much a matter of knowing what not to read as of knowing what to read" (*Spiritus* 12). Frye's ideas about literature developed and expanded through absorption of the central insights he found in other scholars and thinkers. He had a remarkably assimilative mind, and was able to break down and digest great lumps of material, carefully synthesizing everything he read into his own unified vision of literature and culture. He recalls reading, particularly in his younger days, "with tremendous intensity," and of "soaking myself into the book so that I became a part of it and it became a part of me" (qtd. in Cayley 3). What he found useful he seamlessly adapted and moulded to his own coherent framework.

Of special interest to Frye was the work of critics who were interested in myth as a structure of imagery. A good example is Colin Still's fascinating if somewhat eccentric book on patterns of ritual initiation in *The Tempest*; first published in 1921, it was an important influence on Eliot's *The Waste Land* (Eliot mentions it in his preface to Wilson Knight's *The Wheel of Fire*). Written approximately 50 years after his discovery of the book, Frye's essay on the same play contains aspects of Still's intriguing analysis of the purgatorial imagery and theme of ascent, woven flawlessly into his own argument. In developing his encyclopaedic system, Frye himself, to borrow Eliot's phrase, never abandoned anything *en route*. In a letter to Frank Kermode in 1967, he remarks on the latter's description of his system as "mnemotechnical": "It has occurred to me that my overall critical structure is in many respects very like a classical memory theatre" — a system, that is, for assimilating, categorizing, and recalling relevant material.[8] Nothing is ever thrown out once it has found its context: if useful, it is stored, and then (for the system is never finished but always completing itself) recycled, refined, redirected, reshaped within an ever-developing comprehensive understanding of culture and literature. Not surprisingly, one of the things Frye admiringly stresses about Shakespeare is his "scholarship," by which he means his ability to cannibalize, with as little show as possible, a great variety of sources. Nor is it surprising that Frye should confess to having "gone through a long period in which every publication of mine was followed by neurotic fears of being confronted with proof of having plagiarized it from some source I had not read — or, worse still, had forgotten having read" (*Spiritus* 13).

In such a light, it is always instructive to keep track of what Frye *was* reading. One critic I have just mentioned in passing is Wilson Knight, a colleague at the University of Toronto, who, Frye later acknowledged,

> influenced me more than I realized at the time. . . . Like most students of my generation, Knight's books had much the effect on me that Chapman's Homer had on Keats, and the method indicated, of concentrating on the author's text but recreating it by studying the structure of imagery and metaphor, seemed to me then, and seems to me still, the sort of thing that criticism is centrally about. (*Spiritus* 12–13)

Knight had opened *The Wheel of Fire* with a bold rejection of evaluative criticism, and thus anticipated Frye's attack on value judgments in the "Polemical Introduction" to the *Anatomy*. Frye's studies of the poetry of individual poets, such as the book on Eliot and the five essays he wrote on the structure of imagery in the poetry of Yeats and Stevens,[9] not to mention the much more ambitious *Fearful Symmetry*, are very much the enactment of Knight's idea of systematically recreating a work "by studying the structure of imagery and metaphor." Indeed, Frye turned the idea, only crudely developed in Knight's hands, into a revolutionary method. Frye was also intrigued by the work of Knight's brother, Jackson Knight, whom he met in England on his way to Oxford in 1936. Knight's study, *Cumaean Gates: A Reference of the Sixth Aeneid to the Initiation Pattern*, an examination of themes of descent and return, is obviously related to Frye's interest in certain archetypal structures to which he returned until the end of his career.

Frye has spoken more than once of the influence of two authors in particular: Spengler and Frazer. His use of both shows how he drew on the insights even of those authors who, as he rather ungratefully puts it, "seemed extraordinarily limited and benighted in general intelligence and awareness of their world" (*Spiritus* 111). What made them valuable was that "they were both literary or cultural critics, without realizing it, and as soon as I got this clear my conception of the real area covered by the word 'criticism' vastly expanded." Spengler was one source for Frye's organic and cyclical conception of literary history as presented in the *Anatomy* through his series of modes, extending from the mythic to the ironic. Spengler also confirmed and helped to shape Frye's sense of the organic unity of a culture, for he "showed how all the cultural products of a given age, medieval or Baroque or contemporary, form a unity that can be felt or intuited, though not demonstrated, a sense of unity that approximates the feeling that a human culture is a single larger body, a giant immersed in time" (*Spiritus* 111).[10]

Frazer sparked Frye's imagination in the same improbable way. Frazer was "a Classical and Biblical scholar who thought he was a scientist because he had read so much anthropology, and hence was subject to fits of rationalism, which seemed to have attacked him like a disease" (*Great* 35). This "rational *tic douleureux*" prevented him from understanding myths as anything more than " 'mistaken explanations of phenomena, whether of human life or of external nature.' This was obviously part of an ideology designed to rationalize the European treatment of 'natives' on darker continents, and the less attention given it now the better" (38). The tone of impatience with Frazer's ideology reflects Frye's characteristic impulse: to separate the fruit from the tares and go straight to the imaginative seed that redeems even those works that most suffer from the prejudices of their cultural moment. Frye observes that *The Golden Bough* "is by no means as fundamentally wrong and full of holes as some anthropologists and classicists say," and "is still a very valuable book" because of the extraordinary glimpse it offers into "the informing role of mythology in literature" (*Myth* 90). In his plodding and monotonous descriptions of the myth of the dying god, Frazer had unwittingly stumbled upon those patterns of the death and rebirth themes which, liberated from their magical and ritual context, are essential to a deeper understanding of the persistence and significance of literary conventions.

The enthusiasm of Frye's youthful response to Frazer's work is reflected in a letter to Helen Kemp:

> And I've started to read *The Golden Bough* for my Old Testament. . . . It's a whole new world opening out, particularly as that sort of thing is the very life-blood of art, and the historical basis of art. My ideas are expanding and taking shape so quickly that they frighten me; I get seized with terror sometimes that somebody else will think them out before I do, or that I shan't live long enough to complete anything. I shan't live very long in any case, of course; but that doesn't matter if I make the contribution I seem destined to make.[11]

This is the voice of a man pregnant with vision, uncertain of the final form it will take, and horribly anxious about its safe delivery into communicable form, fearful that something might interrupt the birth of what Frye, at the age of 22, was already convinced would be a comprehensive and coherent system for the study of literature.[12] The 20-year struggle that went into his first two major works involved, among other things, bringing the menacing chaos of his ever-expanding interests under control. He speaks in similar terms of how, while writing the *Anatomy*, "endless tantalizing vistas opened up on all sides, yet I had to close my eyes to them, as Ulysses closed his ears to the sirens, because exploring them would get my main thesis out of proportion" (*Spiritus* 12). This stressful sense of chaos was a necessary stage. Frye was attempting to bring to fashion a coherent and all-inclusive vision of what to every other critic seemed the chaotic jumble of works that make up Western culture and literature. His efforts to claim possession of a unified system would culminate first in *Fearful Symmetry* and then in *Anatomy of Criticism*. But he had to be patient. For many years he would speak of the imminent "arrival" of his work on Blake, a work which apparently grew autonomously, coming to completion only in its own good time.

Emotionally, the years in the thirties were for Frye an intense and difficult period of growing attachments and agonizing separations. His relationship with Helen Kemp was fraught with a series of painful physical separations over several years. He had met Helen in his second year at Victoria. Her father was Stanley Kemp, a commercial artist and an acquaintance of the Group of Seven. Her degree in art history led her overseas for a year of study at the Courtauld Institute in London and to a promising career at the Art Gallery of Toronto (now the Art Gallery of Ontario), where she was hired as a lecturer by Arthur Lismer. When Frye became securely established at Victoria, however, Helen resigned from her position. Though she worked for the *Star Weekly* during the war and for a period helped out as an art editor at the *Canadian Forum*, over the years, with Frye's growing fame and the escalating demands on his time, Helen "became much less publicly active" (Ayre 196).

Separation from Helen only added to the discomfort of the solitary and disillusioning time that Frye spent on a mission field on the prairies in the summer of 1934. It was a genuine test of his pastoral mettle, and he failed miserably. The experience gave him a good taste of what he later described as the terror of Canada's non-indigenous inhabitants when faced with the indifference of physical nature:

If I were a mystic, this last week — and probably the coming week too — would register as my dark night of the soul. I'm as miserable as I can be, which is saying a good deal. . . . I'm really all right, you know, but I do feel depressed. I daren't think of four months and a half, or I'd fly into a passion, and I daren't think of anything in Toronto, or I'd go insane. I had a horrible spell of claustrophobia looking over the prairies this afternoon. . . . It isn't exactly a rolling country here, it's more of a fitful, tossing country. The grasshoppers just began to raise hell last year, and are starting in in earnest this year, and everyone is feeling depressed. So I have to cheer up soon.[13]

Part of Frye's depression stemmed from his anxiousness to be with Helen. He wrote to his future wife of his intense desire for marriage, for "real friendship of constant contact," and of how "God himself seems to fade away on these grim prairies: not that He is far away — I never feel that; but He seems curiously impersonal. That, of course, is largely because I left Blake at Stone, the nearest piano a mile away and you in Ottawa."[14] The conjunction in the one sentence of Blake, piano, and Helen (at the time training at the National Gallery in Ottawa) clearly reflects the nature of the fundamental attachments in his life at this time. Indeed, the Geoffrey Keynes edition of Blake, the piano, and his memory of Helen were all Frye had to keep him together that summer. His physical clumsiness, "innate shyness, total ignorance of farming and inability to make small talk" made him terribly ineffective as a student minister (Ayre 98). "That silly mission field!" he wrote to Helen in England the next year, "I feel more resentful and silly about that all the time, when I consider what it did to me."[15] His social isolation, combined with the bleak and dusty landscape, the absence of cultural pursuits, and the narrow-minded repressiveness he encountered, made him thoroughly unhappy. In a letter to his cousin, Frye commented on the "religious problem" he found among his parishioners as

> bound up with the cultural deadness. What these poor people use for literature, art and music is to me the source of the whole evil that makes them regard religion as a social convention rather than an experience. I admire and respect the people in themselves. . . . But they work too hard, and get too little out of their work. (qtd. in Ayre 101)

Already apparent in his thinking at this time is a view essential to his liberal understanding of culture: that the fulfilment of

FIGURE 4

*Northrop and Helen Frye, on their wedding day,
at Emmanuel College, 24 August 1937.*

work, as he was to put it later in *The Great Code*, is play, in the sense of "energy expended for its own sake," "the exhibition of what the work has been done for" (125). The conspicuous absence of such playful exhibition and fulfilling release of energy was perhaps what most depressed Frye as he observed the life led by the hard-working people of the Saskatchewan prairies.

Helen and Frye were separated again when Helen pursued her studies in London. In a letter written in 1935, he informs her that he has stuck her photograph "in a particularly tricky part of the Four Zoas," as though she and Blake were meant to form a composite significant other: ". . . somehow I feel as though I couldn't work on such an absolutely sane, gloriously vital human being as Blake at all unless in some mysterious super-chemical way you belonged."[16] The two were apart again when Frye spent a year at Oxford. On his return, at the end of the summer of 1937, they were married, and Frye taught for a year at Vic in 1937–38. The next year he completed his degree in English literature at Merton College.

Frye's two years at Oxford were in some ways a disappointment, for the intellectual stimulation was less than he had hoped for. The exhilarating part of his stay there was the time spent pub-crawling and travelling with fellow students from overseas, such as Mike Joseph from New Zealand and Rodney Baine from Mississippi. According to Joseph, it was Frye, and not their lecturers, to whom fellow students often looked for inspiration:

> He was already knowledgeable about Blake and Spenser, and was throwing out critical concepts like the "anatomy," which he developed later. Or he would, for example, in talking about *Romeo and Juliet* say: "It's built (making a shape with his hands) like an arch — Escalus is the corner-stone" — and this would be a whole new way of looking at the play. (qtd. in Ayre 131)

As Joseph's reminiscence shows, for all Frye's anxieties and struggle, the years 1934–39 were a decisive period in his intellectual development. In his letters to Helen Kemp there is a tremendous energy, an exuberance alternating with a certain despair that seemed to stem largely from restless anticipation of what was to be his life's work.

In a letter written in the spring of 1935, Frye expresses his frustration with his attempts to give coherent expression to his growing vision of literature. He describes himself (he is 22 at the time) as

> a great yowling infant, having more or less gone through a process described by our mutual friend Mr. Blake:—
>
> I strove to seize the inmost form
> With ardor fierce and hands of flame,
> But burst the crystal cabinet,
> And like a weeping babe became—
>
> A weeping babe upon the wild,
> And weeping woman pale reclined,
> And in the outward air again
> I filled with woes the passing wind.

— but I'm growing up, don't you think I'm not. I've got tremendous ideas, but they're like the myths in primitive religions, huge but monstrous, not consolidated, disciplined or defined. Only the Blake — I know Blake as no man has ever known him — of that I'm quite sure. But I lack so woefully in the way of subtlety. I haven't got a subtle mind — only a pounding, driving bourgeois intellect. I don't insinuate myself between two factors of a distinction — I push them aside; if I meet a recalcitrant fact, I knock it down; which doesn't get rid of it, but puts it in a different position.[17]

In the same letter, Frye speaks of his "criticisms" as being really "synthetic recreations," a phrase that suggests the influence of Wilson Knight's recreative critical method and is a perfect description of his procedure in *Fearful Symmetry*. One of the most common criticisms of the book — for Frye a measure of its success — is that it is impossible to separate the author's ideas from Blake's. The "synthetic intellectual," as he describes himself in the same letter to Helen, is "a critical capitalist": "The English conquered India, the largest, richest, most complicated empire in the world, with a handful of soldiers. I can sail into Blake or Shakespeare or St. Augustine or the Christian religion or aesthetics with two facts and a thesis, and I can conquer it." When Frye speaks of his lack of subtlety and his "pounding, driving bourgeois intellect," it is a colourful way of describing what, in retrospect, can be seen as the relentlessly systematic and encyclopaedic tendency of his criticism. For all the apparent reckless arrogance of the language, the metaphors of conquering and empire vividly capture his method of unifying his central insights and the mass of empirical detail into a global system. In another letter to Helen in 1937, Frye speaks of the seventeenth-century poet Fulke Greville, and of how "it would take at least a month's solid work to read all of him and tie him all up in a neat little sack."[18] Hugh Kenner, recalling his graduate-student days in the forties, reports that Frye, in response to a question about how he would explain a particularly puzzling image in *The Waste Land*, glibly remarked, "I haven't had time to figure that out yet" (qtd. in Ayre 201). Frye's description of his Titanic struggle with Blake is in the same totalizing vein: "I've spun the man around like a teetotum. I've turn him into tiny shreds and teased and anatomized him with pincers. There isn't a sentence in the whole work that hasn't gone through purgatory."[19]

The apparent arrogance of Frye in these early years stems from the excitement of a young man whose central insights are still too embryonic to be communicated effectively. "Consequently I'm damnably lonesome, intellectually," the long letter of 1935 continues. "In conversation, I take up most of my positions through intellectual arrogance rather than reasoned conviction, and consequently won't back out of them." Roy Daniells and Wilson Knight, he claims, are the "only two people in Toronto who have the remotest idea of what I'm talking about . . . and Knight won't read Spengler, Roy won't read Shakespeare, and neither one will read Blake. . . ." Sensing an impasse in the gulf between his ambitions and what he judged at the time to be the limited possibilities of "criticism," he felt that he must "reckon with another side to me, the creative side. . . . You're not working with realities, but with phenomena: go write a novel. A few years ago the challenge was even more uncompromisingly direct: go preach the gospel. . . ." He even wondered then if he should not have "gone into music."

The tension at this moment of his life is reflected in the initially exasperating relationship he seems to have had with Edmund Blunden at Oxford. The two made a rather incongruous marriage of teacher and student. Blunden had all the stereotypical affable obtuseness of the gentleman scholar, but he was not a particularly serious intellectual or critic, and was slow to recognize the genius and intellectual power of this prodigy from the colonies whom he found on his doorstep. He gradually came to admire Frye, and was delighted with his success. The latter's frustration with Blunden, with whom he often felt he was wasting his time, made him privately disgruntled and even scornful, though with his later success his normal good will and magnanimity returned. The two remained in touch, and Frye sent Blunden a copy of the Blake book when it appeared; he even nominated Blunden, in 1966, as an honorary fellow of the Modern Language Association.

Frye's other nagging concern through these years was his position at Victoria College, which remained uncertain because of the apparent reluctance of what he perceived to be an unreasonable and incompetent administration. Eventually, on 20 June 1939, at the end of his studies at Oxford and on the eve of his tour of Italy with Helen, he was made a member of the permanent staff by the Board of Regents. Frye returned to Toronto in the fall of 1939, secure at last in his teaching position: "The train got into Toronto the day the Soviet-Nazi pact was signed, and the next day one of my colleagues who taught the eighteenth century signed up, so I had that course to do as well as the three that I'd been assigned. Preparing for lectures really took all of the energy I had" (*In Conversation* 50–51).

Fearful Symmetry

For some years, Frye's main goal had been to complete the book on Blake. Teaching and the great amount of occasional writing that he undertook continued to delay his progress. If we cal-

FIGURE 5

The author of Fearful Symmetry, *1947.*

culate from the famous seminar in Herbert Davis's course in 1934, it took Frye thirteen years to complete *Fearful Symmetry*. A lot of agony had already gone into it when it was rejected by a subsidiary of Random House in 1943, and Frye felt deeply bitter, doubting himself and the value of a manuscript which seemed so stubbornly unmanageable.

When Kathleen Coburn, a colleague who was soon to gain eminence as the editor of Coleridge's notebooks, went over the manuscript with Frye, she criticized it for its unorthodox scholarship. In her view, the absence of footnotes and supporting documentation only made the often brilliant but sprawling commentary all the more difficult to digest. That Frye took her advice is evidenced by the presence of copious endnotes in the published work. However, his habit of scant conventional documentation, whatever problems it caused, was a sign of the all-encompassing scope that enabled him to unify his subject and recreate the material that shaped his view of Blake. As I have mentioned, readers of the book have remarked on the difficulty of knowing where Frye's commentary ends and Blake's poetic thought begins. In the end, such complaints, which Frye later had the enviable luxury of ignoring, seem pedantic, and are the inevitable resistance of less imaginative practitioners of a discipline to a revolutionary reorientation of its central tenets.

Frye tried and failed to have the book published three times, until it was accepted by Princeton University Press in 1945. In March of that year, Frye sent the manuscript off, describing it as a "complete systematic interpretation of Blake's poetry and symbolism." The chief editor at the time was Datus Smith, who sent it to Carlos Baker (then a Shelley scholar and later to become famous as a Hemingway critic and biographer). Baker's report was largely favourable, but the reservations and suggested revisions anticipated the characteristic objections Frye's work was to encounter in the future, reflecting a prejudice deeply rooted in English studies against a systematic approach to literature.

After the manuscript was revised, it was accepted by the Press in the fall of 1946. When the book came out, it was highly acclaimed. The most dazzling review was perhaps Edith

Sitwell's unrestrained celebration in the *Spectator*: "It is a book of great wisdom, and every page opens fresh doors on to the universe of reality and that universe of the transfusion of reality which is called art" (qtd. in Ayre 205). The success of the book established Frye as a major scholar and consolidated his growing reputation at the University of Toronto.

It was a reputation already large among his students at Victoria, for his authority in the classroom had already given birth to rumours of a hidden king. As an undergraduate in the forties, Don Harron remembers hearing "a great deal about him from Vic senior students," "early Frye-ites" who "kept telling me they were looking forward to the publication of his first book" ("Memory" 19). He describes the first impression he had of Frye, a memorable "vision of an angel in a brown suit":

> Frye was pointed out to me as he was strolling across the campus on a late fall afternoon. It may have been the Rembrandtian lighting; the effect was something I will never forget. He was wearing a brown suit, but the colours that stood out were the pale gold of his hair and the pink of his complexion. Despite the fact that he was at the time 30 years old, he looked to me like one of the cherubs in a painting by Raphael. ("Memory" 19)

Within the next twenty years, this "glad day" of the college was to find himself occupying the centre stage: Frye was to become chair of the Department of English at Victoria College (1952), shortly thereafter principal of the college (1959), and finally chancellor (1978) of the very institution with whose administration he had himself been at such odds as a young scholar in quest of a secure teaching position. His own sense of ironic detachment from his rapid rise is reflected in the wry opening to his installation speech as principal of Victoria College: "I am a little startled to find myself being installed; I would have thought that an honour reserved for more massive pieces of equipment, like presidents and refrigerators."

Later, he would have to contend with even more awkward tributes: the fact that the building he entered every morning to reach his office bore his name, that a bust of himself gravely

FIGURE 6

Principal of Victoria College, 1959.

guarded the stairway to the main lobby, and that every time he wanted to use the Victoria University Library he would find staring out at him from across the reading room a painting of himself, in apotheosis, seated in mid-air above a vast landscape.

Cosmology and Vision

Curiously, the one historical period that Frye could be said to have neglected in his own writings was that of the Middle Ages, and yet its importance to him is manifested, however diffusely, throughout his work. In his travels in England, France, and Italy, he made a point of investigating the great religious art of the medieval cathedrals. The imagery in diagrammatic scenes of the Last Judgement and of the Wheel of Fortune particularly impressed him. Their visual impact was vital to his understanding of the imagery in Blake's poetry and engravings, and they suggested the shape of his unifying scheme in the *Anatomy*, the story-wheel of the four *mythoi*. Frye was keenly interested in the way in which the medieval or Renaissance world-picture, or "topocosm," is essentially a mythology or, in its spatial or visualized form, a cosmology. It is no accident that he valued authors with a special affinity for cosmology, such as Dante, Milton, Blake, Yeats, and Eliot, as well as scholars with a similar bias. Two particularly important ones come to mind, both medievalists interested in the iconography of a culture as a system of codifiable symbols and conventions of interpretation: C.S. Lewis — one of the few lecturers Frye made a point of hearing at Oxford — whose works *The Discarded Image* and *The Allegory of Love* are essentially cosmological studies; and Émile Mâle, whose work *The Gothic Image* is a detailed study of the iconography of religious art in thirteenth-century France.

In Frye's view, to understand a culture one must be able to visualize it as a unified mythological framework that takes a cosmological form. According to Frye, the medieval conception of the cosmos, which remained in force into the eighteenth century, consists of four main levels, two above our own, one below it. The highest level is heaven, the place of the presence of God. . . . Level two is the earthly paradise or Garden of Eden. . . . Level three is the world of ordinary experience we now live in. Animals and plants seem to be well adjusted to this world, but man, though born in it, is not of it: his natural home is level two, where God intended him to live. Level four is the demonic world or hell, in Christianity not part of the order of nature but an autonomous growth, usually placed below ground. (*Secular* 97–98)

One of the first things that Frye notes about this cosmological scheme is its hierarchical structure, moving from top to bottom, like a pyramid, its ideological adaptation being the social and political structure of feudalism. In the structure of authority that is an integral part of the pre-Romantic cosmos (the mythological universe of Dante, Spenser, and Milton), the particular authority of the poet or artist, and of human creativity in general, is derived and secondary: it is nothing in itself, but something only inasmuch as it serves to reinforce the higher cultural authority of religion, morality, and learning. The authentic models of human civilization, the Garden (of Eden) and the City (of God, or Jerusalem), have been established by God, not man. Frye points out that in the modern era some poets have shown a conservative nostalgia for this authoritarian cosmology, and advocate some kind of return to it. It is, for example, precisely such a chain of authority that holds together the structure of imagery in Eliot's work and, in a less imaginative and more pernicious way, the ideology of his reactionary cultural views: in Eliot's view of culture, initiative is seen as coming from an upper transcendental realm and extending downward, according to a kind of "trickle down" theory.

With this cosmology in mind, Frye is able to account for the revolutionary shift that takes place during the period of Romanticism, where what dramatically begins to emerge "is a four-level cosmos that is very like the older one upside down" (*Words* 248). In Frye's view, this revolution in poetic thought is fully realized for the first time in Blake's prophetic poetry, which presents us with the shape of the open and more loosely co-ordinated cosmology that we now inhabit. For Blake, as for modern writers and artists in general, the initiative comes from below, from that which the structure of authority has excluded and repressed, the "point of identity where human creation and imaginative power start, often symbolized as under the earth or sea, like Atlantis" (248). The authority, which before was God's as creator, is now shifted to the poet or artist — in other words, into the hands of humanity itself, a divine being in human form, a Titanic figure whose complete awakening and realization is the prophetic story of history. This figure is a fourfold form of diverse aspects, in which the legs, the lowest part physically, are metaphorically identified with the human creator. The new cosmos "has as its two middle orders the cyclical repression and rebellion against repression which are the worlds of Urizen and Orc respectively. Below Orc is Los, the creative spirit of prophecy and the hero of Blake's later poems. Above Urizen is the alienating sky-god of outer space, Satan the death-principle" (249).

Years later, Frye chose as a frontispiece for *The Great Code* a reproduction of one of the engravings for Job, a depiction of God speaking from the whirlwind and displaying the monster Behemoth to his servant: "Behold now Behemoth which I made with thee."

God's showing of the creation to Job, who looks down on what is now revealed to him, points to the necessity of detaching oneself from one's environment in order to see it as something created. Giambattista Vico's axiom, to which Frye returns throughout his career, is the guiding principle here:

The discoverer of the principle that all verbal structures descend from mythological origins was Vico, and Vico's axiom was *verum factum*: what is true for us is what we have made. But the phrase is less simple than that rendering of it may suggest. What is true for us is a creation in which we have participated, whether we have been in on the making of it or on the responding to it. We are accustomed to think, rather helplessly, of whatever presents itself to us objectively as reality. But if we wake up in the morning in a bedroom, everything we see around us that is real, in

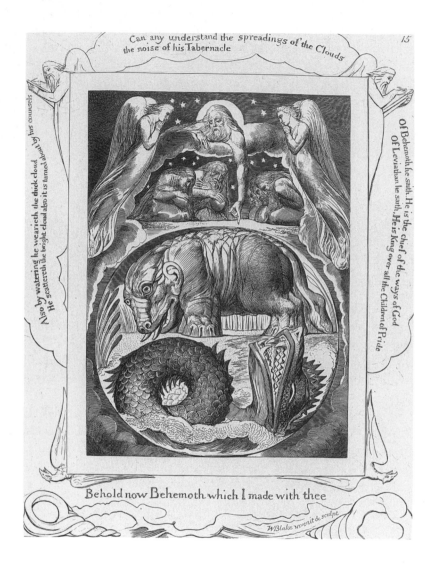

Can any understand the spreadings of the Clouds
the noise of his Tabernacle

15

Also by watering he wearieth the thick cloud
He scattereth the bright cloud also it is turned about by his counsels

Of Behemoth he saith, He is the chief of the ways of God
Of Leviathan he saith, He is King over all the Children of Pride

Behold now Behemoth which I made with thee

W Blake invenit & sculpt

FIGURE 7

Frontispiece to **The Great Code,** *Blake's illustration
of God speaking from the whirlwind to Job.*

48

contrast to our dreams, is a human creation, and whatever human beings have made human beings can remake. (*Words* 82)

If history is a nightmare it is because human beings have made it so, and thus the corollary is true: we have the power to awaken from that nightmare by means of our own creative powers.

Thus, one of the things that drew Frye to Blake was the poet's understanding of the cultural role of poetry and art as an educational force in which "the artist demonstrates a certain way of life; his aim is not to be appreciated or admired, but to transfer to others the imaginative habit and energy of his mind. The main work of criticism is teaching, and teaching for Blake cannot be separated from creation" (*Stubborn* 161). The same point is made in the introduction to *The Great Code*:

> The teacher, as has been recognized at least since Plato's *Meno*, is not primarily someone who knows instructing someone who does not know. He is rather someone who attempts to re-create the subject in the student's mind, and his strategy in doing this is first of all to get the student to recognize what he already potentially knows, which includes breaking up the powers of repression in his mind that keep him from knowing what he knows. (xv)

In Blake's engraving, God speaks out of the whirlwind and, in true teacher style (with the help of an outstretched finger), indicates the created world to the overwhelmed Job, the subject being "the climax of the Book of Job, when Job says: 'I have heard of thee by the hearing of the ear; but now mine eye seeth thee'" (*Myth* 96). The basic function of the teacher is, analogously, to lead the student to revelation, to the point at which she or he is able to *see*, "every breakthrough in education [being] a breakthrough in vision" (*On Education* 13).[20] If the goal of teaching is thus enabling the student to *see* the structure of an area of knowledge — whether it is nuclear physics or ancient philosophy — it is hardly surprising that, in his classroom efforts to visualize his subject for others, Frye soon became famous for madly covering the blackboard with diagrams.

Similarly, Frye understands theory as something close to its etymological meaning *(theoria)* of a viewing or contemplation, and he understands thinking in diagrams or in schemes not as something imposed from without, but rather as inherent in poetry itself. Indeed, harkening after Blake's combination of poetry and engraving, where the narrative is broken up into intense, contemplative moments of picturing, the visualization of an idea is the very basis of what Frye sees as the first step of criticism. Analagous to the aforementioned idea of a detachment in which one views one's environment as something created, the critical act of viewing means that a work or body of work is seized as a complete entity and seen as a "simultaneous conceptual pattern" *(Stubborn* 163). Such a pattern can be grasped only after the spell of reading has been broken and the reader is in possession of the complete work. Stepping back, one can *see* the total design, which is now revealed or discovered. Ultimately, this moment of revelation is to be understood in terms of the *apocalyptic* nature of poetry and art, and is analogous to the Last Judgment in the Biblical narrative, apocalypse having the etymological meaning of unconcealment, of a veil being removed to disclose what lies behind. What is revealed for us by the poet or artist, what he or she intends for us to see by the work or poem is, according to Frye, the metaphoric pattern of imagery as something simultaneous, unfolded, and spread out in space. Our customary dichotomies are thus false and misleading, for the artist, the critic, the scholar, and the teacher all have the same goal: to give us vision.

Even as a student, as I have noted, Frye saw the classroom as a forum to test out his theories, not just for their value, but for their communicability, which for him was perhaps the most important token of their worth. In his lifelong "search for acceptable words," he was committed to developing ideas that would be accessible to a wider audience outside the university, and the later public-lecture format in which so many of his books were born reflects the desire to communicate to a wide, non-specialist public. Not surprisingly, one of the things that depressed Frye about Oxford was the "rather bad" lecturing he

FIGURE 8

Frye at the blackboard (date unknown).

found there, which seemed to consist of little more than "an endless niggling over minutiae and in hopeless disproportion to the very general scope of the course."[21] In light of his later reputation as an educator, it is ironic that Frye's abilities as a teacher should ever have been doubted by his supervisors, who seemed to assume that his precociousness as a scholar disqualified him from the intellectual mediocrity regarded as essential in an effective instructor.[22] Frye was to be actively involved in educational matters throughout his life, and he "had considerable influence on the planning of curricula in English and on the teaching of English in elementary and secondary schools throughout the United States and Canada" (Widdicombe).[23] But for his students, it was his presence in the classroom that left its mark. Margaret Atwood's reminiscence of her first encounter with Frye as an instructor is particularly evocative:

> I don't know what I was expecting: thunder, perhaps, or a larger-than-life talking statue. What actually appeared was an unassuming, slightly plump and rumpled figure, with distracted hair and extremely sharp eyes behind Dickensian spectacles. This person placed one hand on the desk in the front of him, took a step forward, took another step forward, took a step back, took another step back. While repeating this small dance pattern, he proceeded to speak, without benefit of notes or text, in pure, lucid, eloquent, funny and engaging prose, for the space of an hour. This was not a fluke. He did it every week. ("Communicator")

Anatomy of Criticism

By the time Frye had finished grappling with Blake and had worked out "a unified commentary on the prophetic books," he was already well on his way to a "unified commentary on the theory of literary criticism" (Stubborn 160). As he notes in retrospect, "the progress from one interest to the other was inevitable, and it was obvious to anyone who read both books that my critical ideas had been derived from Blake" (160). This accords with the underlying principle of the *Anatomy* that if we are to develop a theory of literature it is one that will derive from the structure of literature. If a single work or the corpus of a single author has a discernible pattern of imagery that can be visualized by the critic, the same must be said of literature conceived of as a whole. In order to understand anything, we are in need of a framework; if we want the whole picture of literature, so to speak, we need a global framework as the final context in which a single symbolic unity must be placed. It is this global framework, "the embodiment of the whole of literature as an order of words, as a potentially unified imaginative experience" (171), that is the vast subject of the *Anatomy*. The work began as a study of Spenser, which was the project Frye submitted for a Guggenheim Fellowship in 1950: "I thought at first of writing my second book on Spenser, but the pull of contemporary literature was too strong and the theory of literature too chaotic, and I was drawn to a more general and theoretical approach which ultimately became the *Anatomy of Criticism*" (*Bush* viii).[24] Appearing exactly ten years after *Fearful Symmetry*, the four essays that comprise the book set out in painstaking detail the framework of interpenetrating contexts in which literature might be understood.

The first two essays deal, in a very broad way, with aspects of literary history. In the context of Frye's life's work, these two essays represent an important step in his ongoing effort to elaborate a coherent theory of the development of verbal culture. One of the incidental targets of Frye's "Polemical Introduction" to the *Anatomy* was documentary criticism, which competed with New Criticism as the most common method of literary analysis. Literary history was practised by social historians who explained literature in terms of the background of the period in which the author lived. In Frye's view, this deplorable situation reflected a failure to address the nature of the authority of poetic communication, which allowed a work to continue to speak to the concerns of readers across history, and not just to the historically limited anxieties of its day. Thus, any understanding of literary history had to be based on something more than social history. Frye's belief in the autonomous authority of verbal culture led him to seek a context for the discussion of literary history which would belong to the nature of literature itself. If words, to borrow from the title of his last major work, have a power of their own, then verbal culture has a life, and therefore a history, distinct from the parallel sequence of historical events.

Two thinkers in particular inspired Frye in formulating his understanding of the historical development of a culture. I have already mentioned Spengler and his conception of the cyclical growth and decline of cultures. Absent in Spengler, however, is an adequate vision of culture as something created by human beings and distinct from the order of nature. As we have seen, it was Vico who, in Frye's judgement, was the first thinker to view the forms of a society's belief and mythology as a human projection. Vico saw human culture as progressing through five stages of growth and decay: the bestial, the age of the gods, the age of heroes, the age of men, and, finally, a decline and plunge into the darkness of barbarism. This historical descent is manifest in the outlines of Frye's modal sequence of five stages, which are defined by the growing decline in the hero's power and freedom of action. In the age of myth, we tell the stories of gods, whose power and freedom of action is unlimited; in the age of romance, the hero is superior, but only in degree, to other men and to his environment; in epic and tragedy, the hero is superior in degree to other human beings but not to his environment; in the age of realism or the low mimetic, the hero becomes a character, and is "one of us," superior neither to other men nor to his environment; finally, in the ironic age, the character, in power and freedom of action, is inferior both to ourselves and to his environment.

In the second essay, Frye applies a similar scheme to the symbolic modes of literary works, which move, now in an inverse order, through literal, descriptive, formal, archetypal, and apocalyptic stages. The pull in literature away from myth toward more realistic and ironic forms of fiction or language involves what Frye calls *displacement*: the adaptation of myth to increasingly realistic rules of narrative plausibility. However, Frye does not see this movement as ultimately a de-mythologizing one. The final context of all fictional modes, even the most realistic, is the shaping power of myth. The bleakest vision in an extremely ironic work of literature, for example, only affects us because it presupposes the ideal of a better world. Myth is not something that human society outlives: social conventions, laws, and fundamental values can be sustained only by imaginative vision, which gives mythological expression to human existential concerns.

In the *Anatomy*, Frye also established the two main verbal categories to which he continued to turn as the organizing principles of poetic thought throughout his career: metaphor and myth. These are the two roots of all verbal culture for Frye. The first essay treats aspects of myth or story (character and setting), and is followed by the discussion of symbolic modes and metaphoric forms of identity in the second essay; the third essay opens with a consideration of the metaphoric structure of imagery, and then proceeds to a discussion of myth as the basis of narrative structure.[25] The opening section of chapter three examines archetypal imagery according to a cosmological scheme, "the general scheme of the game of Twenty Questions, or, if we prefer, of the Great Chain of Being, the traditional scheme for classifying sense data" (140). The vegetable, animal, and mineral worlds provide us with the apocalyptic images of the Garden, the the Sheepfold, and the City, respectively. These are the "organizing metaphors of the Bible and most Christian symbolism," and in their extension they account for the structure of imagery in Western literature. Frye's discussion of imagery here is preparatory to the most influential section of the *Anatomy*, the elaboration of the four *mythoi*, or story types: comedy, romance, tragedy, and irony.

An important influence in Frye's quest for a unifying narrative principle was the group of classicists writing in the early decades of this century, Gilbert Murray, Francis Cornford, and Jane Harrison, whose analysis of Greek rituals based on the myth of the dying god revealed the structure of tragedy and comedy. The overall scheme of Frye's sequence of *mythoi* in the *Anatomy* is adapted from Murray; his theory of comedy owes much to Cornford's work *The Origins of Attic Comedy*. The myth of the "dying god," as Frye and his sources understand it, is the myth of an agricultural community: the dying god is a god of fertility, identified with the vegetation that disappears in winter and returns in the spring. Similarly, Robert Graves's theme in *The White Goddess*, a work to which Frye returns throughout his career, is the story of an earth or nature goddess: the mother, bride, and destroyer of her male consort, a fertility god, who is sacrificed and lamented at the end of each year.

If there is a centre of the *Anatomy*, it is the description of the four *mythoi* in terms of a complete story, whose logic derives from ritual. The circle of *mythoi* is contained in the arche-story of the dragon-killing theme:

> A land ruled by a helpless old king is laid waste by a sea-monster, to whom one young person after another is offered to be devoured, until the lot falls on the king's daughter: at that point the hero arrives, kills the dragon, marries the daughter, and succeeds to the kingdom. (189)

For Frye, the ritual content of such a story is connected to the myth of the dying god, and this myth has four aspects — *agon*, *pathos*, *sparagmos*, and *anagnorisis* — which correspond to the four *mythoi*, or arche-plots, that are the radicals of all possible stories. The *agon*, or conflict, corresponds to romance, which is the sequence of adventures undertaken by the hero. *Pathos*, or suffering and death, corresponds to tragedy and the mutual death of hero and monster. *Sparagmos*, or "tearing to pieces," corresponds to the disappearance of the hero in irony and satire. And *anagnorisis*, or discovery, corresponds to comedy and the recognition of the resurrected hero, who rises in triumph with a new society forming around him (see *Anatomy* 192). In Frye's view, the logic of the structures, conventions, and patterns of imagery in literary works is derived from the complete form of this myth, which, found in a variety of forms in Western mythologies, always manifests the same general shape: the disappearance and return of a divine being. The various story forms in literature, then, are episodes, adding up to one complete story (which often we can only infer and hypothetically reconstruct). One of Frye's favourite illustrations of the importance of a story's shape is the Gospel narrative, in which the tragedy of Christ's crucifixion must be seen only as an episode in a larger comic structure which is resolved in a final rebirth and recognition scene.

The elaborate and detailed analysis of rhetoric and genre, in the fourth and last essay, is difficult to summarize. Frye isolates four root genres in literature, which he ascribes to different verbal rhythms: epos, or the rhythm of recurrence; prose, or the rhythm of continuity; drama, or the rhythm of decorum; and lyric, or the rhythm of association. For a more specific analysis, he turns to the previous discussion of *mythoi* and charts the specific forms of epic, prose, drama, and lyric as they appear at different points on the story wheel.[26]

One form that Frye examines in this last essay — anatomy — he obviously found well suited to his own schematic and diagrammatic form of prose. Anatomy is a satirical genre, which Frye defines in the glossary to his own "anatomy" in the following way: "A form of prose fiction, traditionally known as Menippean or Varronian satire and represented by Burton's *Anatomy of Melancholy*, characterized by a great variety of subject-matter and a strong interest in ideas" (365). Frye carefully outlines the significance of its place in the development of what we now know as the novel (the other three radicals being confession, romance, and the nineteenth-century novel of personality). His attention to the anatomy is one important dimension of his criticism that has been generally neglected and overlooked (see Dolzani). Long before anyone in North America had even heard of Mikhail Bakhtin, Frye had singlehandedly unearthed the literary form of Menippean satire. It was the subject of the first article he wrote, "The Anatomy of Prose Fiction," which appeared in the spring of 1942 in the *Manitoba Arts Review*, a journal founded by Roy Daniells. Frye's early interest in satirical form was, in fact, more than academic. As an undergraduate, he was notorious for his scripting of "The Bob," a series of skits produced by sophomores at Vic lampooning the faculty and frosh; his early fictional writings (dating from 1938 to 1940), which appeared in *Acta Victoriana*, Victoria College's student literary magazine, and the *Canadian Forum*, were all in the satirical mode. Indeed, in his twenties he was still uncertain as to whether he would be a satirist in the cause of social reform or a literary critic. In 1939, when he was irked by the apparent reluctance of the Victoria College administration to offer him an appointment, he proclaimed defiantly (in a letter to Helen) his intention to reform the world with the corrosive power of his pen: "I've got the stuff of an unusually good writer in me, and the sooner I get established as one the sooner I can start defending people. . . . I know how to make fools of people, and I don't want to be absolutely dependent on a sycophantic college."[27]

Everyone who knew Frye, of course, remembers his "flashes of spontaneous wit" (Harron), and readers of his work are familiar with sudden explosions of this wit in his prose. In his correspondence, his great sense of humour is often unrestrained; the letters he wrote to Helen in the thirties, when he was perhaps at his most frank and unguarded, are often outrageously hilarious. Eleanor Cook, a colleague at Victoria College during his later years, remembers seeing "him regularly at high table for lunch: a benign, avuncular figure, who invariably ate ice cream for dessert. Only the voice gave pause — that dry, mild, precise considered speech, with the flat Maritime cadences so well suited to deadpan humour or (had he chosen) deadly irony" ("Northrop" 18). Michael Dolzani suggests that Frye's famous shyness was partly due to a wariness about removing the muzzle and baring a wit "sometimes sharp enough to cut glass" — a protective measure natural enough in someone isolated by the power of an exceptional intelligence — and that his conversation, when he was at ease, tended to reveal the keen edge of a "humour just short of dangerous. As a young man, Frye had a sense of humour at times nearly as irreverent as Blake's, an exuberantly tigerish wit barely held in check by urbanity and the horses of instruction" (Dolzani 66, 59).

Influence and Reaction

The *Anatomy* placed Frye's theoretical views at the centre of a growing interest in critical and literary theory in the fifties and sixties. The work represented a radical challenge to the schools of criticism then dominant, especially New Criticism and documentary criticism. By arguing so persuasively in favour of an autonomous framework for the study of literature, and by demonstrating the possibility of achieving a unified view of such a complex subject, Frye threw into question the ultimate value of the more restricted existing methods. It was, indeed, the limited usefulness of such methods on their own that had driven Frye to write the book in the first place: "The world of criticism was inhabited by a lot of people who were pretty confused about what they were doing, and didn't particularly mind that they were confused. . . . It was just a matter of just being fed up with a field that seemed to have no discipline in it" (*In Conversation* 70).

Not surprisingly, the *Anatomy* came under heavy attack. Indeed, a good indication of its importance was the outrage it provoked in critics who continued to defend the entrenched interests of isolated, inadequately theorized, and unsystematic critical methods. At the height of the controversy that followed its publication, Frye ironically muses in a letter to Harold Bloom expressing his regret at having missed the latter's paper at the English Institute: "I rather got the impression that my presence there would have instituted an unwarranted interference with freedom of speech."[28] Many readers were bewildered by the unprecedented systematic and encylopedic ambitions of the work; intimidated, they dismissed it as some sort of "unusually elaborate sequence of classifications, an edifice resembling some gigantic purple-martin-house" (Dolzani 60). Typical of the tendency to see in Frye's systematizing little more than extraordinary but sterile ingenuity was the New Critical proponent W.K. Wimsatt, who snidely remarked, "Superimposed fourth-of-July pinwheels, with a reversing sequence of rocket engines, may give a dim idea of the pyrotechnics involved here" (103). He judged the structure of Frye's system to be "divided between truism and *ad libitum* fantasy" (99). It is a criticism that Frye himself seems to have anticipated in his own doubts about his work. In 1935, in a letter to Helen, he remarks, "I can draw blueprints for the loveliest castles in the air. . . . This is a work of art, creative in essence. It's silly to object that these castles won't stand up if they were built. Who said anything about their standing up?"[29] The difference, of course, lies in the twenty years that separate those honest doubts from the careful realization of the system that Frye as a young scholar had only begun to intuit.

In a letter to Harry Levin over a decade after publication of the *Anatomy*, Frye concurs that the title of the book, though "admittedly more saleable," tended to raise "irrelevant problems."[30] The idea of an anatomy evoked the unpleasant image of a heartless critic unfeelingly dissecting a cadaverous body of knowledge. Like the reservations outlined in Baker's assessment of *Fearful Symmetry*, the specific doubts expressed in Douglas Bush's otherwise highly favourable reader's report anticipated the sort of objections that unsympathetic readers would continue to raise. Bush questioned what he saw as the book's view that "literature is a series of patterns constituting a verbal universe which exists to provide materials for the super-sophisticated critic's solitary games," concluding that such a verbal universe was "inhuman and stifling" (qtd. in Ayre 250). The book's original title, "Structural Poetics," reflected the true contextual spirit of the *Anatomy* as a work attempting to provide a coherent system for the study of poetic structure. It was changed only at the insistence of Princeton University Press, which seemed to share the assumptions of a scholarly audience still haplessly rooted in a sentimental and short-sighted misconception of Frye's goals. Frye was to discover in the coming years, in the controversial response to his own work,

how strong and immediate the emotional overtones of the word "system" are in this fragmented age. Jail-building, pigeonholing, providing a glib answering service for under-graduates, overweening ambition on the part of the system-builder, are some of the readiest associations. In the muddled mythology of stock response, the system-builder is the spider who spins nets out of his bowels, as contrasted with the bee who flits empirically from flower to flower and staggers home under his burden of sweetness and light. ("Reflections" 136)

The very aspects of Frye's work that critics had the most trouble accepting were precisely what made his work most prophetic of the radical advancements in continental critical theory that would have such an enormous influence on literary studies in North America and England. Indeed, structuralist critics such as Tzvetan Todorov and Gerard Genette were to recognize the obvious relevance of his ideas to intellectual developments in France, and in Italy he was viewed as a celebrity. Today, the continuing relevance of the *Anatomy* to semiotics and cultural criticism is a further indication of the extent to which Frye's view of literature and culture was, and perhaps in certain aspects remains, well ahead of its time.

It is important, however, to stress the heuristic quality of Frye's exposition. Like any useful diagram or scheme, the system is there for the purposes of demonstration and insight, and is not an end in itself. Labels like comedy or romance, as Frye insisted more than once, should be thought of as *context* words: they are intended only to provide a basis for discussion of the narrative structure of particular literary works, and they are not an attempt to reduce the unique meaning of all stories to the same meaning, or to a single, inflexible scheme. Frye later defined the context more in terms of "something like a magnetic field, a focus of energy, not a farmer's field with a fence around it" (*Myth* 81). One of the most common criticisms is that his system denies the uniqueness of the reader's experience of original literary works. Frye would be the first to insist that the experience of literature is primary and must precede the act of critical detachment; however, as he points out, the unique is precisely what criticism cannot address, just as the unique is what the biologist, who is interested in the laws of species and phylum, can never hope to know. Nonetheless, it can be argued that in the course of the intricate and detailed discussion of each of the four *mythoi*, for example, by virtue of the complex distinctions that his encyclopedic system allows, Frye succeeds quite well in giving a sense of how the uniqueness of individual works can be analyzed in detail as a function of context.

The most loaded and invidious attacks on the book and on Frye's ideas in general only served to indicate their importance and extraordinary influence: 100,000 copies of the *Anatomy* were sold over the next 25 years. With its publication, Frye had become the undisputed cynosure of literary criticism in the English-speaking world. His work was widely celebrated and became extremely influential. A gauge of its importance is the 1964 seminar of the English Institute, which chose the *Anatomy* as the topic of discussion by a panel composed of Angus Fletcher, Murray Krieger, and Geoffrey Hartman — in their early days all Frye aficionados — with the dissenting Wimsatt to present the minority view. In his letter of invitation to Frye, who chose, with characteristic delicacy, to absent himself, the chair of the seminar, R.W.B. Lewis, described him as the "most powerful critical force in English-language critical activity today. This is why we believe that any meditation on the present condition of criticism is inevitably a meditation on the present state of the critical principles you have stood for and exemplified."[31]

In the next two decades, Frye published 14 books. Many of them are collections of essays on diverse subjects, and much of the work in this period is a development of ideas introduced or outlined in the *Anatomy*. The two companion studies of Shakespearean comedy and tragedy, *A Natural Perspective* (1965) and *Fools of Time* (1967), along with the later study of the problem comedies, *The Myth of Deliverance* (1983), expand on core insights of chapter three of the *Anatomy*. *The Secular Scripture* (1976) is a trans-historical exploration of narrative as it is structured by the form of quest-romance discussed in the same chapter, and *The Well-Tempered Critic* (1963) develops further some of the observations on genre found in chapter four of the *Anatomy*. All of these books display the welcoming and communicative style for which Frye became famous. Indeed, his works have the pleasurable rhythm of heightened conversation about them; all at once an unexpected but carefully prepared turn in the argument pulls the reader up with the recognition that he or she has, unwittingly, attained a new and exhilarating perspective. Frye, as Margaret Atwood observes,

did not write for other critics . . . he wrote instead for the intelligent general reader. . . . Pick up any of his books and what you will hear . . . is a personal voice, speaking to you directly. Because of its style, flexiblity, and formal elegance,

FIGURE 9

*Colleagues at Victoria College presenting him with
the Festschrift* Centre and Labyrinth, *1983.
From left to right: Eleanor Cook, Chaviva Hosek, Northrop Frye,
Judy Williams, Julian Patrick, Patricia Parker.*

its broad range and systematic structure, his literary criticism takes its place easily within the body of literature itself. ("Communicator")

Frye has spoken frequently of the freedom that comes only from great discipline, but that seems like ease and natural grace. It is this sense of "final freedom of movement" born of "incessant discipline and practice" (*Great* 125) that pervades his prose. His fully developed style of exposition is not an indifferent vehicle of thought, but a well-crafted instrument of vision and revelation.

Canadian Literature

In 1950, in the midst of his work on the *Anatomy*, Frye was asked by "J.R. MacGillvray, then editor of the *University of Toronto Quarterly*, to take over the annual survey of Canadian poetry in its 'Letters in Canada' issue which had been made by the late E.K. Brown" (*Bush* viii). For a decade, Frye was to find himself in the delicate position of evaluating a literary tradition that was only just coming into its own. Canadian literature, in which Frye had shown a deep interest from his very earliest days, thus became an important testing-ground for the fully developed critical principles set forth in the *Anatomy*. Frye had grown up "in two towns, Sherbrooke and Moncton, where the population was half English and half French, divided by language, education and religion, and living in a state of more or less amiable Apartheid" (*Bush* v). Consequently, he was sensitive to the unique tension and cultural diversity of the country, and recognized "that a sense of unity is the opposite of a sense of uniformity" (vi). However, Frye's early view of Canadian literature was uncompromising and often unflattering. He saw it as the expression of an immature culture, there being "no Canadian writer of whom we can say what we can say of the world's major writers, that their readers can grow up inside their work without ever being aware of a circumference" (214).

In retrospect, Frye's opinion of his reviews of Canadian poetry was that

the estimates of value implied in them are expendable, as estimates of value always are. . . . For me, they were an essential piece of "field work" to be carried on while I was working out a comprehensive critical theory. I was fascinated to see how the echoes and ripples of the great mythopoeic age kept moving through Canada, and taking a form there that they could not have taken elsewhere. (viii–ix)

Indeed, Frye's view of Canadian literature was to change dramatically by the end of his life. With the emergence of internationally acclaimed writers, such as Atwood, Findley, and Munro, he came to recognize that Canadian culture had at long last awakened "from its sleeping beauty isolation" (*On Education* 7). He would even go so far as to say that "this maturing of Canadian literature . . . is the greatest event of my life, so far as my own direct experience is concerned."

It was, indeed, a direct experience, for he helped to bring that literature to adulthood. As a teacher, he came in contact with many of the young writers of a rapidly maturing literary culture. Frye, however, was never, as Margaret Atwood remembers, "an 'influence' in the traditional sense. . . . He had no interest in producing a Frye school of writing, or any other form of cookie-cutter clone of himself" (Tribute 7). What he did do was to take

the whole business seriously. He did not consider the arts a frill, but a central focus of a healthy society. . . . Lord help us, he even used to read *Acta Victoriana*, the Victoria College student literary magazine. If you published something in it, you were likely to get stopped outside Alumni Hall for a muttered but incisive comment or two, addressed to your shoes. (7)

As a critic, Frye's particular sensitivity to formal and generic concerns "conferred freedom upon the artist to follow her or his own lights," and part of that freedom came from his efforts

FIGURE 10

*Frye with George Ignatieff (Chancellor of the
University of Toronto) and Margaret Atwood
(recipient of an honorary degree),* 1983.

to help readers see what it was that they were reading. We all know the doggerel poem about critics: "Seeing an elephant, he exclaimed with a laugh, What a wondrous thing is this giraffe." Perhaps one of his greatest gifts to writers was his lifelong work to ensure that if you created an elephant, it would never again be mistaken for a giraffe. (7)

It was this same concern with genre and literary convention, the insight that behind the individual work of literature stood a shaping "order of words," that enabled Frye to provide the first comprehensive view of the Canadian literary tradition. Like so many of his other ideas, his views here were formed early and remained essentially unchanged: an essay on "Canadian and Colonial Painting" appearing in the *Canadian Forum* in 1940 already contains his central insight into Canadian art as a response to the natural environment. Carl Klinck approached Frye to help edit what was to become *Literary History of Canada* (1965), and his conclusion to the volume represents his most complete formulation of Canadian literary and cultural history. The piece, in four parts, begins by outlining the historical, social, political, and economic factors that have helped to shape the "Canadian sensibility," a sensibility "profoundly disturbed, not so much by our famous problems of identity, important as that is, as by a series of paradoxes in what confronts that identity. It is less perplexed by the question 'Who am I?' than by some such riddle as 'Where is here?' " (*Bush* 220).

Frye observes that the early literature of Canada's European inhabitants is marked by a "garrison mentality," a protective and hostile attitude reflecting a "deep terror in regard to nature" (225). He further relates this sense of solitude — the experience of the isolated individual or parochial community of being surrounded by a menacing environment — as linked to the important tradition in Canada of the "arguing intellect" (227), of partisan, rhetorical, and ideological argument. The latter is opposed to the "disinterested structure of words" (228) in poetry or fiction, and its dominance was a sign that Canadian literature did not yet constitute a unique tradition but was in large part somewhat sub-literary. The Canadian writer had the difficult task of adapting the highly organized body of European verbal culture to what was essentially an alien natural environment. She or he had to create a tradition of fiction and poetry in a cultural context not entirely conducive to it, one which, because of this sense of solitary adversity, tended to favour realism over romance. "The conflict involved is between the poetic impulse to construct and the rhetorical impulse to assert, and the victory of the former is the sign of the maturing of the writer" (231). Frye's point is that for a mature literary tradition to develop, imaginative writers must detach themselves from the natural and social world out there and find their "identity within the world of literature itself" (238).

One obstacle to such a detachment was the deeply rooted perception in the Canadian literary tradition of the natural world as something unconscious, indifferent, and even hostile to human concerns. The problem is that such a vision of nature is finally a projection of the unconsciousness and the death-wish in human beings themselves. For Frye, the first poet to emerge from this tradition and show signs of a mature vision was E.J. Pratt, "with his infallible instinct for what is central in the Canadian experience" (*Bush* 226). In Pratt's poetry, we are witness over and over again to the struggle of human dignity in the face of this death-wish in nature and man, perhaps most dramatically set forth in *Brébeuf and His Brethren*. When Canadian poets begin to find their identity in the world of literature, what they envision is a recreation of nature, a social and natural world transformed according to the models of the City and the Garden projected by the poetic imagination.

In the embryonic Canadian tradition, this depiction of the heroic struggle of the solitary individual or group against a terrifying natural environment contained the seeds of what Frye calls the pastoral myth, with its social ideal of "the reconciliation of man with man and of man with nature" (249). This ideal represents the return of the repressed vision of innocence associated with childhood, which tells us that the objective world is ultimately a lie and that the invisible world of the imagination is what is real; it is the "quest for the peaceable kingdom" (249) that Frye speaks of in the closing passages of that essay, and that he finds in Edward Hicks's painting depicting the Messianic prophecy of Isaiah, with its

"haunting vision of a serenity that is both human and natural"
(249).

Concern and the Bible

In the mid to late sixties, Frye quite naturally began to shift his focus to the theory of culture and society. There was an atmosphere of growing social crisis, largely focused on the Vietnam war, and the university had become a place of contestation and controversy. Frye suddenly found himself in the role of resident cultural mandarin associated with a stabilizing wisdom and authority, and for a period he was "harried and bedevilled by different requests to make oracular pronouncements on student unrest."[32] Ironically, Frye's response to the radicalism of the sixties appeared to put him in the conservative camp. As the former principal of Victoria College and as a recognized figure of cultural authority, he found himself to be an uncomfortably conspicuous target of attack. His humour, however, rarely failed him. In a letter to Harry Levin in 1972, he wryly notes that "a group of local Maoists on the campus [held] a meeting on my birthday with the general theme of 'let's all hate Norrie Frye.' I don't know how many they got, and I'm sure they didn't know that the day had any connexion with me. But it's always nice to be remembered."[33] In a sometimes maddening defence of the university and culture, he would counter with what he himself chose to call "a bourgeois liberal view" (*Double* 9). This description of himself as the proponent of a classical liberal position, with its possible suggestion of a capitulation to the status quo, is deceptive, and reflects, more than any growing complacency on his part, a significant change in historical context. "The position of the 'new left' today is very different. The typical radical of today does not think of himself as primarily a 'worker': he reflects rather the disillusionment of a consumer-directed economy, the so-called affluent society" (*Divisions* 158). At its worst, Frye detected in the student movement's call for "relevance" in education a disturbing echo of the Nazi educational policy of *Zweckwissenschaft*,

FIGURE II

*Northrop Frye, University Professor at
the University of Toronto, 1967.*

or "target knowledge" (*In Conversation* 153). The danger that he saw in the movement's manifest lack of direction and its often reckless tactics was its possible "connexion with the fascism of a generation ago, a similarity which confuses many people of my generation, whose 'left-wing' and 'right-wing' signposts point in different directions" (*Divisions* 159).

In this atmosphere of public controversy, he began to articulate what he would come to call the myth of concern, the idea that

> Myths are expressions of concern, of man's care for his own destiny and heritage, his sense of the supreme importance of preserving his community, his constant interest in questions about his ultimate coming and going. The poet who shapes the myth is thus entrusted with the speaking of the word of concern which, even though in early times it may often have been a word of hostility and a celebrating of war and conquest, is still the basis of social action. (*Bush* 194)

Beginning with *The Modern Century* (1967), the word "concern" crops up with notable frequency in Frye's work, reflecting an increasing attention to the way that literature and culture relate to the cares and anxieties of human existence. In the closing passage of *The Modern Century*, Frye speaks of a myth of concern as a co-ordinating or unifying set of ideas which inform any culture. If a mythology takes a religious or political form, and gains institutional authority — for example, Christianity or Marxism — it tends to become a closed structure of belief, and concern then becomes, in relation to change, a form of anxiety, of "a conservative, or let's-be-careful-about-losing-what-we've-got" variety, in contrast to "a radical, or let's-clear-out-all-this-stuff-and-have-a-fresh-breeze-blowing-through, anxiety" (*Divisions* 156). With Romanticism, the hitherto predominant, largely Christian myth of concern and its structure of authority begins to be replaced by a more open and loosely structured mythology. As we have seen, in Frye's scheme, the social significance of the Romantic revolution is that human beings themselves begin to assume responsibility for the creation of a world that makes human sense. The modern mythology we now inhabit, if "not as well unified as the earlier one," is still a mythology, that is, "a structure built by human concern: it is existential in the broad sense, and deals with the human situation in terms of human hopes and fears" (*Modern* 113). Finally, distinct from verbal culture or cultural mythology as the embodiment of a structure of belief, there is the language of concern that we find in literature and art. At the end of *The Modern Century*, Frye concludes that the identity we should be concerned about "is the one that we have failed to achieve," which "is expressed in our culture, but not attained in our life" (123). Here, culture is identified with the creative works of the human imagination, as we find them in poetry, literature, film, and art.

In the spring of 1968, Frye gave a public lecture at Cornell University in which he elaborated the notion of concern in relation to Shelley's "Defence of Poetry." In response to the lecture, Harold Bloom wrote Frye expressing the

> wish that you would write an essay expanding the myth of concern, as I think a good many of us, as well as myself, need to read it. . . . I've read *The Modern Century*, and see some of its relevance. But, if I understand your recent work, perhaps you need to write another essay on just the myth of concern itself.[34]

The book that Frye came up with is *The Critical Path*, "a farce," as he describes it, "in the etymological sense: a fifty-minute lecture stuffed with its own implications until it swelled into the present monograph" (7). It is very much a transitional book, a bridge between the ideas that led to the grand synthesis of the *Anatomy* and the emergence of ideas that culminated in the two great books on the Bible. Frye was to remark in a letter to Harry Levin three years after its publication that "that book was, as you recognized, the most personal one I have written, and consequently it is a book that leaves me very vulnerable on all fronts."[35]

In it, Frye develops further the distinction between concern as a closed structure of belief and concern as it appears in literature and art. The distinction is between the historical anxieties of a particular period, an aspect of all literary works, and literature inasmuch as it reflects a release from those anxieties, when we see it "in its context as part of the total poem that the human imagination has made" (99). Shakespeare is a favourite example of Frye's, since his plays uncritically adopt the language of concern that belongs to the age of Elizabethan England, with its cosmology structured by the hierarchical Great Chain of Being. At the same time, Shakespeare's works speak a language that carries us beyond the closed structure of belief of his time. Literature, in other words, "represents the *language* of human concern. Literature is not itself a myth of concern, but it displays the imaginative possibilities of concern, the total range of verbal fictions and models and images and metaphors out of which all myths of concern are constructed" (98).

In establishing that the "total subject" of the critic, who must be at the same time "a student of mythology," consists of all those "areas of concern which the mythical language of construction and belief enters and informs" (98), including "large parts of religion, philosophy, political theory, and the social sciences" (98), Frye anticipates the interdisciplinary nature of current criticism, which refuses to divorce literary questions from larger social and cultural ones.[36] Contrary to the common misconception of the *Anatomy* as an impressive but rarefied formal edifice entirely divorced from social concern, Frye's view of criticism is of the widest possible social, cultural, and historical scope, and this view, paradoxically, grows out of the fundamental insight of the book: that the language of poetry and literature has a particular character and authority of its own. Indeed, the enormous social and cultural relevance of literature depends precisely on the non-referential and non-ideological nature of the language of concern that it speaks:

Nobody would accept a conception of literature as a mere dictionary or grammar of symbols and images which tells us nothing in itself. Everyone deeply devoted to literature knows that it says something, and says something as a whole, not only in its individual works. In turning from formulated belief to imagination we get glimpses of a concern behind concern, of intuitions of human nature and destiny that have inspired the great religious and revolu-

73

tionary movements of history. Precisely because its variety is infinite, literature suggests an encyclopaedic range of concern greater than any formulation of concern in religious or political myth can express. (103)

For the "concern behind concern," or what is world-wide or universal in human concern, Frye comes up with the following simple claim: "What is potentially world-wide is an assumption, too broad in itself to constitute a myth of concern, that life is better than death, freedom better than slavery, happiness better than misery, health better than sickness, for all men everywhere without exception" (107).

The formulation of the universal basis of the imagery of concern in literature is something Frye returned to with renewed insight in *Words with Power*. As the book on Spenser turned into the *Anatomy*, so Frye's pursuit of the myth of concern ends up taking the form of his two books on the Bible. His feeling that *The Great Code*, like *The Critical Path*, was "a very vulnerable book" (xii) is an indication of the struggle involved in his thinking during this period. In 1969, in a letter to Bloom, he speaks of gradually being taken over by a

large and complicated design for a successor to the *Anatomy*. . . . The myth of concern is certainly a central part of it, but at present it looks like being the end of it, so it will probably take me a fair time to get there. There may, of course, be various mirages along the way.[37]

The letters of this period are riddled with references to the portentousness of his difficulties. He speaks of having "embarked on a study of the Bible which is blocking up all my time and energy"; of trying to "work on an almost insanely complicated book on the Bible"; of having "to struggle with a large book on the Bible and English Literature."[38] As the ominous language of *agon* suggests, Frye finds himself once again in labour to deliver an essential part of his vision of literature, which (as he notes in the introduction to *The Great Code*), "beginning with a study of Blake published in 1947, and formulated ten years later in *Anatomy of Criticism*, has revolved

around the Bible. Hence the total project is, among other things, a restatement of the critical outlook I have been expounding in various ways for years" (xiv). Indeed, the continuity of this focus can be seen in comments Frye makes to Helen in a letter written almost half a century before:

> I propose spending the rest of my life . . . on various problems connected with religion and art. Now religion and art are the two most important phenomena in the world; or rather the most important phenomenon, for they are basically the same thing. They constitute, in fact, the only reality of existence. . . .[39]

It would seem natural to regard the two eventual books on the Bible, along with, at the other end of his career, *Fearful Symmetry* and the *Anatomy*, as the four pillars of Frye's life work.

The third pillar was raised in 1981, when the long-heralded *The Great Code: The Bible and Literature* was published. In 1948, Frye began teaching a course on the Bible, which he had actually started in 1940 as an informal seminar under the auspices of the Student Christian Movement. It was to become an institution at the University of Toronto, a course that Frye taught for over half a century, ended only by his failing health and subsequent death in January of 1991.

> My interest in the subject began in my earliest days as a junior instructor, when I found myself teaching Milton and writing about Blake, two authors who were exceptionally Biblical even by the standards of English literature. . . . So I offered a course in the English Bible as a guide to the study of English literature, and as the most efficient way of learning about it myself. (*Great* xi–xii)

Frye's immediate assumption about the Bible is that it has a unity, the first operation of the critic being to "begin to formulate a conceptual unity corresponding to the imaginative unity of his text" (xii). For Frye, this is an axiomatic procedure, as the unity conceived of is not one of meaning but of *shape*, since "no book can have a coherent meaning unless there is some coherence in its shape" (xii). The assumption of the unity of

FIGURE 13

In his study at Victoria College, 1981.

the Bible is all the more pertinent in that the Bible "has traditionally been read as a unity, and has influenced Western imagination as a unity" (xiii). Thus the book turns out to be, not surprisingly, the "presentation of a unified structure of imagery and narrative" (xiii).

The opening section on language reprises the discussion in the *Anatomy* of fictional and verbal modes, and anticipates the first part of *Words with Power*. Frye's aim is to supply a framework for the study of the imaginative language of the Bible by placing it within the larger context of the Western tradition of discourse. In his view, there are three main conceptions of verbal meaning in the West. In the epoch we occupy now, the predominant and privileged use of language is largely descriptive; in other words, verbal constructs aim at some sort of equivalence to a world out there, to which they attempt to supply a verbal analogy. This use of language gains definitive authority with Locke and his exclusive reliance on the direct experience, through the senses, of an objective world to which language must try to be faithful. Dominant before this, into the eighteenth century, is the conceptual or metonymic use of language, which aims at producing verbal constructs as analogues to a transcendent spiritual realm. The language of the Bible is different from both of these verbal modes, because the imaginative language it uses is primarily metaphoric and mythic. For Frye, "the literal basis of faith in Christianity is a mythical and metaphorical basis" (*Double* 17). Accordingly, *The Great Code* focuses on the metaphoric and mythic structures of Biblical language.

Frye also introduces here the concept of kerygma, a theological term which means "proclamation," a type of verbal communication peculiar to the Bible. In the Bible, we must think of a channel of communication existing between an Other and human beings, and kerygma refers to that channel when the message is coming from the Other to man, rather than the other way around. "This transforming power is sometimes called kerygma or proclamation. Kegryma in this sense is again a rhetoric, but a rhetoric coming the other way and coming from the other side of mythical and metaphorical language" (*Double* 18).

In *The Double Vision*, Frye turns to the Book of Job to illustrate what he means by this revolutionary use of language. He contrasts the use of language in Elihu's speech, "defending and justifying the ways of God," with the subsequent "proclamation of God himself, couched in very similar language but reversed in direction" (*Double* 18). As we have seen, the paradigmatic significance of this turning-point, in which God speaks to Job from the whirlwind, explains Frye's selection of the Blake engraving as the frontispiece of *The Great Code*: the "reason for basing kerygma on mythical and metaphorical language" is that "such a language is the only one with the power to detach us from the world of facts and demonstrations and reasonings, which are excellent things as tools, but are merely idols as objects of trust and reverence" (*Double* 18).

For Frye, God is first of all the spoken Word, the logos, and metaphor and myth are the forms taken by the message passed from the Other to the human subject, God being "a spiritual Other, not a spiritual object, much less a conceptual object" (20). Typology, then, is the particular form of "revelation" that this transmitted message, or proclamation, takes in the Bible, according to a sequence of phases extending from Creation to Apocalypse, seven in all: creation, revolution, law, wisdom, prophecy, gospel, and apocalypse. Revolution, a phase which in the Biblical narrative extends from Abraham to Moses, is a particularly important one because it shows the vertical direction of the communication and the break in historical continuity that such a proclamation implies. We can see here how the romantic, revolutionary, and mythopoeic basis for Frye's view of literature as a global Word (literature as a body of words that says something as a whole, and not just in its individual forms of expression) is based on this radical understanding of proclamation.

As he promises in his introduction to *The Great Code*, Frye offers an analysis of the unity of the structure of imagery and narrative in the Bible. He supplies a table of Apocalyptic and Demonic versions of "a body of concrete images: city, mountain, river, garden, tree, oil, fountain, bread, wine, bride, sheep, and many others" (xiii), which reflects a chain of being, like Frye's game of twenty questions from the *Anatomy*, composed of an intricate series of categories of images derived from the divine, human, and natural worlds. The overall schema reflects a polarizing and separation of divine and demonic realms. A secular counterpart of this "moral dialectic," as it is called in the *Anatomy*, can be found in Frye's examination of romance in the latter work and in *The Secular Scripture*. The identification of such a dialectical scheme as the structuring principle of Biblical imagery reflects one of his earliest insights: that comic romance is the central structure of Western literature.

The unity of narrative structure in the Bible is immediately observable in the fact that the Bible has a beginning in Creation and an end in Apocalypse. Between these two moments, a narrative ensues, the shape of which, with its series of comic ups and tragic downs, Frye reconstructs in what he playfully calls his "manic-depressive" chart. Frye refers to the chart as "a sequence of *mythoi*," and he emphasizes that "all the high points [e.g., the Garden of Eden, the Promised Land, Jerusalem] and all the low points [e.g., Egypt, Babylon, Rome] are metaphorically related to one another" (*Great* 171). The overall "U-shaped pattern, approximate as it is, recurs in literature as the standard shape of comedy," and Frye views the entire Bible, with its "repeating *mythos*" of apostasy and deliverance, as a "divine comedy" structured according to this narrative logic (169).

Just short of a decade after publication of *The Great Code*, the sequel volume, *Words with Power*, appeared. Like its predecessor, the book opens with a discussion of verbal modes, and of the kerygmatic (proclamation through metaphor and myth) as the pre-eminent mode of the Bible. The emphasis now is on the Biblical structures that have informed the shape of imagery and story in Western literature. Frye locates the unifying structural principle of story and imagery in primary human concerns, which can be divided into four areas: food, sex, property, and freedom. Literature "incorporates our ideological concerns, but it devotes itself mainly to the primary ones, in both physical and spiritual forms: its fictions show human beings in the throes of surviving, loving, prospering, and fighting with the frustrations that block these things" (*Double* 16). From such a simple statement, an entire literary system unfolds. Frye derives four main areas of literary imagery from these "primary throes," and identifies them with four thematic variations or

80

archetypal symbols: cave, garden, furnace, and mountain. These four areas together form a cosmology, structured on the mythological idea of the world-tree, or *axis mundi*.

As Frye is primarily interested in the creative initiative reflected in these areas of symbolism, he borrows his conception of the imagery in the lower half of the scheme, the cave and the furnace, from the inverted topocosm introduced by the Romantic revolution, in which creative initiative comes from below. Correspondingly, his conception of the imagery in the upper half of the scheme, that of the garden and the mountain, is largely derived from the pre-Romantic topocosm in European culture, in which the initiative comes from above. The bottom of the chart is the area that Blake associates with the artist figure, Los; art is ultimately what Frye intends by "property," the expansive energy and consciousness belonging to an imaginative vision of reality, that unseen or invisible world which is the substance of faith. It is this power alone, the power of the arts to "show us the human world that man is trying to build out of nature" (*On Education* 44), that has any hope of delivering humanity from the Orc-Urizen cycle of history, or ordinary world of physical and social reality. In *Words with Power*, we are witnesses once again to the breath-taking consistency of Frye's essential vision, as we find ourselves confronting a four-level cosmos or squared circle, another mandala or fourfold wheel. For we are back in the *Anatomy* and the four contextual story-patterns or *mythoi*: comedy, romance, tragedy, and irony. It is a return with a difference, however, as Frye himself would stress at the end of his life: "For I find myself constantly returning to the assumptions and intuitions of my earliest critical approaches, but the return is not simple repetition, rather continuity into a different life" (8).

Last Words

Frye's fame as a literary scholar took him all over the world. At the end of the seventies there was a flurry of travelling: to Japan in 1977, New Zealand in 1978, and Italy in 1979. The tour of

Speaking at the Italian Congress, 1988.

Italy, where he was greatly admired as a literary theorist, was particularly successful, and he returned to Rome even more triumphantly some years later, in May of 1987, to attend a three-day symposium devoted to his work. On an almost month-long tour to Australia in 1986, he was accompanied by Helen, who for many years had been suffering from poor health. On the eve of their return home, after a long plane flight to Cairns in Queensland, she collapsed and died in hospital. Frye's grief at her death left him depressed and reclusive, and for some time it disturbed the progress of his work on a second study of the Bible. In the summer of 1988, he married Elizabeth Edy Brown, an old Vic classmate and the widow of a former member of parliament from Brantford, James Brown. A friend of the Fryes for many years, she had first met Northrop in their freshman year almost 60 years before, and had worked with Helen at the Art Gallery of Toronto in the thirties.

Revitalized, Frye was able to bring *Words with Power* to fruition. The book appeared in the fall of 1990. Only months later, Frye entered hospital to be treated for cancer, and died suddenly of heart failure on 23 January 1991, at the age of 78.

The Double Vision, "a shorter and more accessible version of the longer books . . . on the relations of the Bible to secular culture" (xvii) was Frye's last work, appearing shortly after his death. The idea of a "double vision" is taken from a verse by Blake. For such a visionary critic, it was a fitting theme for what turned out to be a closing statement. It may be true that "visionary criticism," as Wimsatt suggests, "enjoys not quite the immunities of visionary poetry" (107), but Frye's life work never pretended to be anything but an argument for, not of, poetry. The preface to *The Double Vision* concludes with the calm presentiment of its author's approaching end, unsurprising in its serenity for someone whose life had been lived so completely on so many fronts. Frye warns that the opinions of the book, whose first three chapters were delivered as lectures

addressed by a member of The United Church of Canada to a largely United Church audience . . . represent the opinions of one member of that church only. And even these opinions should not be read as proceeding from a judgment seat of final conviction, but from a rest stop on a pilgrimage, however near the pilgrimage may now be to its close. (xvii–xviii)

If a pilgrim's progress is the obvious metaphor for the spiritual quest of a member of the United Church, it is all the more so for someone who saw the power of Bunyan's great book as rooted in romance rather than doctrine. If romance is a kind of scripture, albeit a secular one, then scripture is perhaps a form of romance, however sacred. Frye has said, "I always wanted to choose and see my path and was convinced that that was what God wanted too, and that if I went on with this 'Lead Thou me on' routine I would run into spiritual gravitation and fall over a cliff" (*In Conversation* 49). In a similar vein, he responds in *The Secular Scripture* to a proverb from Ecclesiastes, "Better is the sight of the eye than the wandering of desire":

> Great literature is what the eye can see: it is the genuine infinite as opposed to the phony infinite, the endless . . . stimulation of the wandering of desire. But I have a notion that if the wandering of desire did not exist, great literature would not exist either. (30)

Nor, presumably, would Frye's great contribution to the life of thought, for it is to both these crucial elements — seeing *and* desire — that he would appear to owe his extraordinarily productive intellectual life: a life devoted to a double vision of words with power, to the world that the eye can see, and to the desire which allows us to see the invisible world that is the reality of the imagination.

FIGURE 15

*Frye with students in his course on the
Bible, Religious Studies 320, 1988.*

Notes

1 See Ayre (25). On page 194 of the *Anatomy*, Frye cites Bunyan's book as, after Spenser's *Faerie Queene*, the best paradigm (in the English literary tradition) of the form of quest-romance, which Frye saw as the root form of the structure of Western literature.

2 For example, in *A Natural Perspective*, a study of Shakespearean comedy, he would note that Shakespeare, "like Bach, was a scholar of the ear" (22) and that "the romances are to Shakespeare what *The Art of the Fugue* and *The Musical Offering* are to Bach: not retreats into pedantry, but final articulations of craftsmanship" (8). Frye's interest in operatic features in the same study is also significant, though more in line with a literary interest in the use of popular dramatic conventions, as an early review article in *Acta Victoriana*, "Current Opera: A Housekeeping," published in 1935, suggests.

3 Ayre notes that Frye's "absorption in books was immediate and so pervasive that in the normal troubled sleep stage of four-year-olds, he awoke one night with a searing image from an illustration in the Altemus edition of *Pilgrim's Progress* of Faithful being burned at the stake" (25).

4 Letter to Helen Kemp, 23 Apr. 1935.

5 Letter to Helen Kemp, 10 May 1934.

6 See Ayre's informative discussion of this episode, 290–91.

7 Here is a particularly distasteful example of Eliot's pernicious view of "culture": "The population should be homogeneous; where two or more cultures exist in the same place they are likely either to be fiercely self-conscious or both to become adulterate. What is still more important is unity of religious background; and reasons of race and religion combine to make any large number of free-thinking Jews undesirable" (*After* 20). Thus, the understandable archness of Frye in the following passage, written in the early fifties when Eliot's influence was at its height, in which he gives voice to the fundamental antagonism of their views:

I have no thought of trying to prefer one kind of English culture to another, and I regard all value-judgments that inhibit one's sympathies with anything outside a given tradition as dismally uncritical. I say only that this combination of Protestant, radical, and Romantic qualities is frequent enough in English culture to account for the popularity, in every sense, of the products of it described above. There has been no lack of Catholic, Tory, and Classical elements too, but the tradition dealt with here has been popular enough to give these latter elements something of the quality of a consciously intellectual reaction. During the twenties of the present century, after the shock of the First World War, this intellectual reaction gathered strength. Its most articulate supporters were cultural evangelists who came from places like Missouri and Idaho, and who had a clear sense of the shape of the true English tradition, from its beginning in Provence and medieval Italy to its later developments in France. Mr. Eliot's version of this tradition was finally announced as Classical, royalist, and Anglo-Catholic, implying that whatever was Protestant, radical, and Romantic would have to go into the intellectual doghouse. (*Fables* 149)

[8] Letter to Frank Kermode, 11 Oct. 1967. The term used by Kermode, "mnemotechnical," involves a reference to Francis Yates's *The Art of Memory*.

[9] "Yeats and the Language of Symbolism" (*Fables* 218–37); "The Rising of the Moon: A Study of 'A Vision'" (*Spiritus* 245–74); "The Top of the Tower: A Study of the Imagery of Yeats" (*Stubborn* 255–77); "The Realistic Oriole: A Study of Wallace Stevens" (*Fables* 238–55); "Wallace Stevens and the Variation Form" (*Spiritus* 275–94).

[10] This last image is, incidentally, a good example of Frye's assimilative style: it is borrowed and adapted from the closing passages of Proust's *A la recherche du temps perdu*, given a Blakean resonance (the idea of the human form divine), and blended flawlessly into his own text.

[11] Letter to Helen Kemp, 19 Oct. 1934.

[12] The birth image is used advisedly. Mildred Shamas, one of his graduate students at the time, reports that Frye, at a party in 1943, alluding to what he then considered to be the successful completion of the Blake manuscript, enigmatically announced with a twinkle in his eye that he had "just had a baby" (see Ayre 186).

[13] Letter to Helen Kemp, 10 May 1934.

[14] Letter to Helen Kemp, 19 May 1934.

[15] Letter to Helen Kemp, 23 Apr. 1935.

[16] Letter to Helen Kemp, 23 Apr. 1935.

[17] Letter to Helen Kemp, 3 May 1935.

[18] Letter to Helen Kemp, 3 Feb. 1937.

[19] Letter to Helen Kemp, 11 Mar. 1935.

[20] Frye tells of his

mother's experience as a teacher in the late eighteen-eighties. One of her pupils was a girl named Susan, who had been nicknamed 'Confusion' by the previous teacher and ridiculed as a dunce. My mother discovered that she was blocked by the theorem in Euclid that the angles at the base of an isosceles triangle are equal. . . . My mother spent most of a day going over this theorem with her: she was a desperately honest girl who would never say she understood something if she didn't, and my mother said that the expression on her face when she finally said 'I see it, Miss Howard' was worth not only the day but her whole career as a teacher. (*On Education* 12)

[21] Letter to Helen Kemp, 27 Oct. 1936.

[22] In 1934, Wilmot Lane informed Frye that he had established his "status as a scholar" at the college: however, Victoria "placed a strong emphasis upon teaching ability and the necessity of getting good instruction across to the undergraduates," and "he had a hard time persuading Brown that I would make a good teacher" (letter to Helen Kemp, 19 Oct. 1934). In 1939, in an exchange of letters between them, W.S. Wallace, then chancellor of Victoria College, responding to Frye, who was expecting an appointment and felt that he would make "a fairly good teacher," implied that the claim was questionable, observing pedantically that "scholarship in a University such as ours, falls short of its full achievement unless the scholar is also a good teacher" (letter from Northrop Frye to W.S. Wallace, 13 Jan. 1939; letter from W.S. Wallace to Northrop Frye, 31 Jan. 1939; qtd. in Ayre 156).

[23] See *On Education*, a collection of essays about the theory of education, written for a variety of occasions, which reflect Frye's lifelong commitment to questions of pedagogy. He was a founding member of the Ontario Curriculum Institute, and wrote the preface to *Design for Learning: Reports Submitted to the Joint Committee of the Toronto Board of Education and the University of Toronto*, ed. Northrop Frye (Toronto: U of Toronto P, 1962) 3–17. He was the author of *On Teaching Literature* (New York: Harcourt, 1972), a monograph written in connection with a series of textbooks for the secondary-school curriculum, and supervising editor of *Literature: Uses of the Imagination* (12 vols. New York: Harcourt, 1972–73).

[24] Ironically, Frye was never to return to "the practical aspects," at least not in the form of a book-length study of Spenser, though the kernel of it is perhaps to be found in the essay "The Structure of Imagery in *The Faerie*

Queene," which appeared in 1961.

25 A similar pattern of analysis appears in *The Great Code*. Frye opens the book with a discussion of myth followed by questions of metaphoric identity, and then in the second part reverses the order in a discussion of patterns of imagery and narrative structure. There is, one might say, a fearful symmetry to the structure of Frye's own thought.

26 One important area of study opened up by Frye is his isolation of the archaic forms of charm and riddle to explain the characteristic associative rhythm of lyric, to which he later devotes a fascinating essay, "Charms and Riddles" (*Spiritus* 123–47).

27 Letter to Helen Kemp Frye, 15 May 1939.

28 Letter of 21 Sept. 1960. The English Institute was an organization of which Frye was a former chair (1953), and with which his first association dated from 1948, when he delivered "The Argument of Comedy," the basis of his discussion of comic structure in the *Anatomy*.

29 Letter to Helen Kemp, 3 May 1935.

30 Letter to Harry Levin, 15 Feb. 1968.

31 Letter to Northrop Frye, 9 Nov. 1964.

32 Letter to Harold Bloom, 23 Jan. 1969.

33 Letter to Harry Levin, 15 Aug. 1972.

34 Letter to Northrop Frye, 27 Jan. 1969.

35 Letter to Harry Levin, 3 Mar. 1972.

36 As A.C. Hamilton remarks, criticism today "is now being recognized as a social science, with literary theory becoming cultural theory, as it is in Frye's post-*Anatomy* writings" (220).

37 Letter to Harold Bloom, 19 Feb. 1969.

38 Letter to Harry Levin, 15 Aug. 1972; letter to Angus Fletcher, 17 Aug. 1971; letter to Martha England, 5 Feb. 1973.

39 Letter to Helen Kemp, 23 Apr. 1935.

Works Consulted

Atwood, Margaret. "The Great Communicator." *Globe and Mail* 24 Jan. 1991: C1.

——. "Tribute: A Service in Memory of H. Northrop Frye." [Convocation Hall, University of Toronto, 29 Jan. 1991.] *Vic Report* 19.3 (1991): 7.

Ayre, John. *Northrop Frye: A Biography.* Toronto: Random, 1989.

Balfour, Ian. *Northrop Frye.* Twayne's World Authors Series 806. Boston: Twayne, 1988.

Cayley, David. *The Ideas of Northrop Frye.* Canadian Broadcasting Corporation, 19, 26 Feb. and 5 Mar. 1990.

Cook, Eleanor. "Northrop Frye as Colleague." *Vic Report* 19.3 (1991): 18.

Cook, Eleanor, et al. *Centre and Labyrinth: Essays in Honour of Northrop Frye.* Toronto: U of Toronto P, 1983.

Cornford, Francis M. *The Origin of Attic Comedy.* Cambridge: Cambridge UP, 1934.

Denham, Robert D. *Northrop Frye: An Annotated Bibliography of Primary and Secondary Sources.* Toronto: U of Toronto P, 1987.

Dolzani, Michael. "The Infernal Method: Northrop Frye and Contemporary Criticism." Cook et al. 59–68.

Eliot, T.S. *After Strange Gods: A Primer of Modern Heresy.* New York: Harcourt, 1934.

——. *Selected Prose of T.S. Eliot.* London: Faber, 1975.

Frazer, Sir James George. *The Golden Bough: A Study in Magic and Religion.* 1922. London: Macmillan, 1963.

Frye, Northrop. *Anatomy of Criticism: Four Essays.* Princeton: Princeton UP, 1957.

——. "The Argument of Comedy." *English Institute Essays: 1948.* Ed. D.A. Robertson, Jr. New York: Columbia UP, 1949. 58–73.

——. *The Bush Garden: Essays on the Canadian Imagination.* Toronto: Anansi, 1971.

——. *Creation and Recreation.* Toronto: U of Toronto P, 1980.

——. *The Critical Path: An Essay on the Social Context of Literary Criticism.* Bloomington: Indiana UP, 1971.

——. "Current Opera: A Housecleaning." Frye, *Reading the World* 1–4.

——. *Design for Learning: Reports submitted to the Joint Committee of the Toronto Board of Education and the University of Toronto.* Ed. Northrop Frye. Toronto: U of Toronto P, 1962.

———. *Divisions on a Ground: Essays on Canadian Culture.* Ed. James Polk. Toronto: Anansi, 1982.

———. *The Double Vision.* Toronto: U of Toronto P, 1991.

———. *The Educated Imagination.* CBC Massey Lectures Series. Toronto: CBC, 1963.

———. "The Emphasis Is on the Individual, the Handful of Shepherds, the Pairs of Lovers. . . ." With Justin Kaplan. Frye, *On Education* 206–11.

———. *Fables of Identity: Studies in Poetic Mythology.* New York: Harcourt, 1963.

———. *Fearful Symmetry: A Study of William Blake.* Princeton: Princeton UP, 1947.

———. *Fools of Time: Studies in Shakespearean Tragedy.* Toronto: U of Toronto P, 1967.

———. *The Great Code: The Bible and Literature.* Toronto: Academic, 1982.

———. Installation Address, Principal, Victoria College. Toronto, 21 Oct. 1959. Canadian Manuscripts Collection, Victoria University Library.

———. Letters. Canadian Manuscripts Collection, Victoria University Library.

———. *The Modern Century.* Toronto: Oxford UP, 1967.

———. "Moncton, Mentors, and Memories." With Deanne Bogdan. Frye, *A World in a Grain of Sand* 323–41.

———. "Music in My Life." With Ian Alexander. Frye, *A World in a Grain of Sand* 269–79.

———. *Myth and Metaphor: Selected Essays, 1974–1988.* Ed. Robert D. Denham. Charlottesville and London: UP of Virginia, 1990.

———. *The Myth of Deliverance: Reflections on Shakespeare's Problem Comedies.* Toronto: U of Toronto P, 1983.

———. *A Natural Perspective: The Development of Shakespearean Comedy and Romance.* New York: Columbia UP, 1965.

———. *Northrop Frye in Conversation.* Ed. David Cayley. Concord, ON: Anansi, 1992.

———. *Northrop Frye on Shakespeare.* Ed. Robert Sandler. Markham, ON: Fitzhenry, 1986.

———. *On Education.* Markham, ON: Fitzhenry, 1988.

———. *On Teaching Literature.* New York: Harcourt, 1972.

———. *Reading the World: Selected Writings, 1935–1976.* Ed. Robert D. Denham. New York: Peter Lang, 1990.

———. "Reflections in a Mirror." Krieger 133–46.

———. *Romanticism Reconsidered: Selected Papers from the English Institute*. Ed. Northrop Frye. New York: Columbia UP, 1963.

———. *The Secular Scripture: A Study of the Structure of Romance*. Cambridge: Harvard UP, 1976.

———. *Spiritus Mundi: Essays on Literature, Myth, and Society*. Bloomington: Indiana UP, 1976.

———. "The Structure of Imagery in *The Faerie Queene*." Frye, *Fables of Identity* 69–87.

———. *The Stubborn Structure: Essays on Criticism and Society*. Ithaca: Cornell UP, 1970.

———. *A Study of English Romanticism*. Chicago: U of Chicago P, 1968.

———. *T.S. Eliot: An Introduction*. Chicago: U of Chicago P, 1963.

———. "War on the Cultural Front." *Reading the World* 282–86.

———. *The Well-Tempered Critic*. Bloomington: Indiana UP, 1963.

———. *Words with Power: Being a Second Study of "The Bible and Literature."* Harmondsworth, Eng.: Penguin, 1990.

———. *A World in a Grain of Sand: Twenty-Two Interviews with Northrop Frye*. Ed. Robert D. Denham. New York: Peter Lang, 1991.

Graves, Robert. *The White Goddess: A Historical Grammar of Poetic Myth*. London: Faber, 1961.

Hamilton, A.C. *Northrop Frye: Anatomy of His Criticism*. Toronto: U of Toronto P, 1990.

Harron, Don. "A Memory of Frye." *Vic Report* 19.3 (1991): 19.

Klinck, Carl F., ed. *Literary History of Canada: Canadian Literature in English*. Toronto: U of Toronto P, 1965.

Knight, G. Wilson. *The Wheel of Fire: Interpretations of Shakespearian Tragedy with Three New Essays*. 1930. London: Methuen, 1960.

Knight, W.F. Jackson. *Cumaean Gates: A Reference of the Sixth Aeneid to the Initiation Pattern*. Oxford: Blackwell, 1936.

Krieger, Murray, ed. *Northrop Frye in Modern Criticism*. Selected Papers from the English Institute. New York: Columbia UP, 1966.

Lewis, C.S. *The Allegory of Love: A Study in Medieval Tradition*. Oxford: Oxford UP, 1936.

———. *The Discarded Image: An Introduction to Medieval and Renaissance Literature*. Cambridge: Cambridge UP, 1964.

Mâle, Émile. *The Gothic Image: Religious Art in France of the Thirteenth Century*. Trans. Dora Nussey. 1913. New York: Harper, 1972.

Saurat, Denis. *Blake and Modern Thought*. 1929. New York: Russell, 1964.

Weston, Jessie L. *From Ritual to Romance.* 1920. Garden City, NY: Doubleday, 1957.

Widdicombe, Jane. "A Biographical Sketch." *Vic Report* 19.3 (1991): 17.

Wimsatt, W.K. "Criticism as Myth." Krieger 75–108.

Yates, Frances A. *The Art of Memory.* 1966. Harmondsworth, Eng.: Penguin, 1969.